VESTIGES OF LIGHT

A MEMOIR OF ABANDONMENT, RESILIENCE, AND HOPE

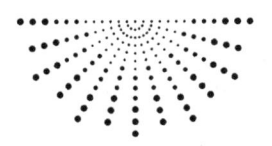

STEPHANIE PLEASANT

SOLANO
PUBLISHING

COPYRIGHT

SOLANO PUBLISHING
Chattanooga, Tennessee

Copyright © 2025 by Stephanie Pleasant

All rights reserved.

No part of this publication may be reproduced, distributed, or transmitted in any form or by any means, including photocopying, recording, or other electronic or mechanical methods, without the prior written permission from Solano Publishing, except as permitted by U.S. copyright law. For permission requests, contact Stephanie Pleasant at VESTIGESOFLIGHT.COM.

For privacy reasons, some names, locations, and dates may have been changed.

ISBN-13s:

- 978-1-969424-00-7 (Hardback edition)
- 978-1-969424-01-4 (Paperback edition)
- 978-1-969424-02-1 (eBook edition)

First edition 2025

DEDICATION

"She needed a hero so that's what she became." - Unknown

Dedicated To

~

Nena, Steppa

INTRODUCTION

∼

"Love me when I least deserve it, because that's when I most need it." - Swedish Proverb

∼

The following memoir is a collection of stories, depicted in chapters — my truth, as it unfolded.

If I am honest with myself, I have known I needed to write much of this book since my early 30s. Like so many, life was too busy, filled with children and work, to take the time and effort to write a book. Besides, I really didn't want to go back there. Daily life had enough struggles, as it was — why would I pile on a heavy load of darkness to the mix? Furthermore, I was not a writer, so how could I take on such a daunting task?

Fast forward to age 58, when I was suddenly overcome with

INTRODUCTION

memories of my childhood and youth. I wasn't sure why the past was haunting me after all these years, but there it was. And it wasn't budging. No amount of projects or prescriptions would make it go away. Months were going by, and I wasn't only being haunted by the memories, but they were hunting me down at every turn. Life was good, and I sure resented the intrusion of these dark, sad, and scary memories. I'd been over a lot of them through the many years. Even with counselors at some points. Why were they badgering me now?

I finally caved and went to see another counselor, an art therapist I had great respect for and trusted. During several sessions, I poured out the life rundown and asked her pointedly, why the hell these memories were trampling me now, when life was feeling good. There was my answer, she told me. Life had finally settled down some, and my mind felt safe and secure enough to allow those feelings to come back up so they could be explained and processed properly. It sounded a little out there to me, but I sat with that conclusion for a while to see what came of it.

Around the same time frame, my gifted astrologer friend, Chris, suggested I was coming into my second Saturn return. "What's that?" I asked.

"Google it," he responded. "It's pretty interesting and actually fits your current predicament pretty well."

One day, the plethora of memories were once again filtering their way through my thoughts, ad nauseam. It was evening, and I was sitting in my spot on the sofa, looking out into the beautiful woods behind our home. One faint streak of light landed on a few leaves of the big magnolia tree in my line of sight. *Vestiges of light,* I thought. *There are always vestiges of light. Sometimes you may need to look for them, but they are always there.*

INTRODUCTION

Light, a symbol of hope, is always close at hand. And with resilience and hope, you can conquer anything that comes your way in life. I realized in that very moment that I needed to purge all the memories by writing this book and I should call it 'Vestiges of Light.'

PART I
THE DIPLOMAT'S DAUGHTER

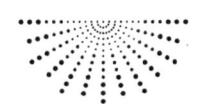

"The one thing I am willing to bet on is myself" - Beyoncé

1
ABANDONED

"Lonely is not being alone, it's the feeling that no one cares."
- Author Unknown

The lingering smell of cigarette smoke, old coffee, and incessant despair tarnished the heavy air. Slumped against the pitted plaster wall, I sank onto the cold, unforgiving concrete floor in the waiting area of the Atlanta Crisis Center. My father left me there with a center counselor, Connie Fulbert. "She's a rebellious, incorrigible teenager," he bitched to her. Then he turned on his heels and was gone.

It was spring 1971, and I had turned 15 a few weeks before. Anxious and confused, I waited for Connie to get off work and figure out what would become of me. I felt distrustful, lost, and ashamed, wondering, *how shitty a person are you when your own parents don't want you?*

A lump formed in my throat, and my eyes bristled, but I fought back the tears, determined to keep my composure and appear stable. As time stretched on, ominous dark thoughts clamored for my attention. Finally, an icy wave of shock washed over me, cradling me in its numbing embrace, dimming the frantic scenes in my mind.

I was vaguely aware of the people shuffling around the front counter, each trapped in their own hell, craving a lifeline. I gazed vacantly through the glass front wall, watching the hippies wander through the midtown strip. Their spontaneity stood in stark contrast to the uncertainty that weighed on me.

How the fuck had it come to this?

2
COLONEL GORDON FLYNN - THE DIPLOMAT AND THE DADDY

"Heroes are ordinary people who make themselves extraordinary." - Gerard Way

My mind drifted far beyond the Crisis Center entrance in futile attempts to piece together the events that led to my current predicament.

My relationship with my father hadn't always been so contentious. In fact, I had been his darling "nena" (colloquial for little girl in Spanish) and he, my absolute hero. I worshiped Daddy.

Gordon Flynn never verbally demanded respect, but he certainly commanded it from all his children, as well as anyone who met him. At a trim 5'8", he didn't possess a formidable figure, yet he cast an imposing presence. We knew we were in the company of a self-controlled genius, his representative aura exuding the sense of an elite, sophisticated gentleman.

The colonel hailed from a large Irish Catholic family in Rome, Georgia. The Flynn family gatherings were lively affairs with chatter, laughter, and glasses full of sherry. Among them was my great Aunt Agnes, a skilled journalist who wrote for the *Atlanta Journal-Constitution*. Great Aunt Hannah, a vibrant New York flapper turned Catholic nun, exuded a sense of purpose and compassion as she helped homeless people and prisoners. And then there was great Uncle Charles, a distinguished attorney whose presence commanded admiration. After World War II, he took on the assignment of sitting on the historic Nuremberg trials. Later, he served as the U.S. Solicitor General and was then appointed to the prestigious United States Court of Appeals in Washington D.C. The life force of the family was intertwined with the memories of these incredible relatives. The general store in downtown Rome, where you could purchase everything from baked goods to women's wear, was the renown Flynn Store. Under the guidance of the Colonel's father, the shop thrived, a testament to his keen business sense and financial acumen. The Flynn Store stood tall and proud on Broad Street. Its original structure still stands today, evidence of its enduring presence. The façade, an attractive blend of gray, brown, and red bricks, emits a sense of history. The raised brick lettering, spelling out "T. Flynn 1895," evokes a nostalgic charm. This building stands as a lasting tribute to the Flynn family's invaluable contributions to the Rome community and its history.

Following in the footsteps of his esteemed Uncle Charles, my father pursued his education at the University of Georgia Law School and established his own private law practice in

Rome. However, when World War II broke out and all were called to serve, he didn't hesitate to shutter his office and enlist in the Air Force, where his career took off at warp speed.

Impressive piloting skills, along with his leadership aptitude, netted him frequent promotions and opportunities to fly a variety of airplanes, including bombers. Over the course of his time in the Air Force, he earned three Distinguished Flying Cross medals and several notable uniform bars and insignia.

I relished hearing my father's stories, especially the ones of his heroics during the war. My most requested tale was of him being forced to land his C-47 plane in the Mediterranean Sea. Nestled beside me in his cozy bed, he would begin the story with a serene and measured voice, evoking the same composure he likely displayed during the harrowing ordeal.

"Nena, during the big war, one of my plane's engines got hit, and we had to crash-land in the ocean. The plane was spiraling, twirling down toward the water — fast. I pulled back on the controls, careful to take the plane out of its spin and get it drifting straight again. The dark Mediterranean Sea loomed ahead as I guided the plane toward the water. After a difficult but successful landing in the sea, I yelled to my fellow servicemen, 'Get the rubber life raft out! Take any supplies you can and get the battery-operated radio!' Only once my men were safely in the raft boat, did I jump out of the airplane and join them. We radioed for help and huddled together in the dark, waiting for rescue. Floating in the shark-infested waters of the Mediterranean Sea for hours, we wondered if we would survive the night. Finally, a U.S. Navy ship in the area reached us and pulled us from the frigid water," my father recited from a well-rehearsed memory. I marveled at the Distinguished Flying Cross he received for his heroic bid to save all of his crew.

The version of events was, of course, adapted for the ears of a young child. The true story proved much more harrowing — a rendering I wouldn't hear until adulthood, and a narrative that would linger with me for a lifetime.

3
EARLY CHILDHOOD - THE ATTACHÉ YEARS

"I good ... I good" - Nena

My father soon received a commission as the Air Force Attaché to Argentina. In 1956, when I was seven months old, we embarked on an ocean liner journey to the capital, Buenos Aires. As our ship arrived and docked, a vibrant scene unfolded before us. Local and regional dignitaries, along with their families and staffs, gathered on the dock, their smiles and waves filling the air with excitement. I reciprocated their greetings with a queen's wave, eliciting a chorus of laughter and joyful giggles from the crowd. The attention fueled my delight, and I continued to entertain my newfound admirers from the safety of my daddy's arms. Years later, I stumbled upon photographs from that day. In the pictures, my parents stood smiling alongside my siblings: my 10-year-old brother, Gordy, Jr., and the 9-year-old twins, Henry and Ivette. The pride on my father's face was unmistakable as he admired his prodigies of perfection.

A young hippie's coins dropping to the floor next to the pay phone jolted me back to my status as a present-day pariah. I had fallen so far from the graces of my father's adulation. *Who must he be trying to get ahold of?* I pondered. *Does he have a family that cares about him?* I walked back time to when it was simpler.

I could still visualize the entire floor plan of the Argentine Attaché house on Avenida Quintana where we lived until I was 4 years old. It was a sprawling, two-story, red brick Colonial style home with a pristine manicured lawn and swimming pool, complete with cabana. We had maids, gardeners, and a chauffeur, Carlos. Probably in his 40s, Carlos was a dapper gentleman, sporting a trim male frame and fine facial features. His professionalism was unmatched, whether standing guard at the front of our home or shuttling our family around town.

Emma was our cook and my live-in nanny. Memories of Emma are coexistent with the taste of white rice mixed with a teaspoon or two of mayonnaise, a combination she fed me that apparently I loved.

Emma was a tall, ample woman, with an olive complexion that concealed her actual age and masked her alcohol habit, which was a common topic of quiet gossip in later years. A tipsy Emma was the norm, and yet she always kept me safe, from what I could remember.

A preschooler in a vast house, I roamed around the place seemingly on my own — or at least so I thought. One of my first memories from those early days happened when I was around age three. I woke up from a nap and made my way downstairs and outside. With a confident tone and my authentic Spanish accent, I told Carlos, "Mama said I could go to Sherry Plier's house to play." He graciously opened the back door to our sleek, black Mercedes and helped me in with a gentle boost.

Upon our unexpected arrival at Sherry's house, her mother looked quizzically at Carlos as he explained we were there for my playdate with Sherry. Following a phone call home, it was agreed that I could stay and play with Sherry, and Carlos would come back later to pick me up. I don't recall receiving any consequences for this clever antic, but I assume someone told Carlos never to depend on my three-year-old word again.

My early memories seemed so benign, like when my mother enrolled me in ballet lessons. I loved to dress up in tutus and dance around the studio. I would arrive home from classes and share my dancing prowess with my parents, who gushed with pride at my skills, lacking though they might have been.

How self-conscious can you be at three? And why? I thought as I recalled the small day school I attended on weekdays. We often went swimming in a plastic kiddie pool, all of us in underwear. I felt funny about us all being in underwear — why, I don't know, as my playmates seemed completely oblivious.

I could also recall one gala my parents hosted at our home. Dignitaries from all over South America were in attendance. Our home was buzzing with sharply dressed men in military regalia and women in elegant gowns. Servers passed around cocktails and silver trays of fancy foods in tuxedos and bow ties. The conversations flowed effortlessly and smiles abounded. The elegance and reverence exuding from the rooms enchanted me.

Despite the formality of the evening, or perhaps because of it, my two much older brothers enlisted me to pull one of their pranks. "Shrimp," as they affectionately called me, "go down the stairs and yell out to the crowd, 'MONKEY!'" Obediently, I walked down the stairs in my little footie pajamas, peeked over the railing, and yelled as loud as I could, "MONNKEEYYY!!!" The crowd turned just in time to see me flee back up the stairs. My siblings were overjoyed, laughing uncontrollably, and I took great pleasure in successfully fulfilling their wishes. I'm pretty sure my brothers received a stern lecture for this antic.

The family moved back to Washington, D.C. in 1960, when I was four. We traveled there on the Moore-McCormack ocean liner, an absolutely magical cruise for an active and adventurous four-year-old. My older brothers and sister, Gordy now 14, and Henry and Ivette 13, watched over me, and keeping up with me would soon prove to be a challenge for them. Two seconds with eyes averted and I would take off. One time, I ducked under the guardrails and got to the edge of the deck so I could get a better view of the dolphins swimming beside our massive ship. I watched in awe as these majestic creatures soared in the air and swam in seeming synchronicity. Within minutes, I felt hands lifting me up, and I was firmly admonished for having passed the security rails. My siblings waited behind the bars as the boat-hand passed me back to them, along with a lecture on safety for all of us.

I made a new friend with a boy my age when I saw him sitting alone in the front row of the on-board movie theater. I left my seat next to my brother, Gordy, to go sit next to him. It wasn't long before we were kissing each other as if we were on a big date. I felt so grown up and special. Before I knew it, Gordy's powerful arms squeezed my shoulders, lifting me above the seat back and carrying me out of the theater. "You don't do that with boys or anyone, do you hear me?" Gordy chastised harshly. His disapproval of my kissing my new friend left me mortified and bewildered. However, the message conveyed through Gordy's reaction struck a chord within me, triggering a sudden realization that reverberated through my senses. The disgrace. The guilt. The all-important appearances. I was so ashamed of myself for disappointing Gordy and making him mad at me. He was my eldest brother and my hero, next to Daddy, of course.

"Yes, operator, I'd like to make a collect call," the change-spilling hippie said on the phone. "Yes, make it from Matt." His demeanor changed and his shoulders relaxed when he heard the voice on the other end of the line. "Hi, Mom, yeah, I'm ok. No, really, I'm fine," he whispered. "You don't need to worry about me. Things are looking up for me. Yeah, I think I might be getting some work soon. Landscaping work with a cool guy I met." After a quick response from his mother, he said hastily, "Hey, Mom, I need to get going. I've got people here waiting to use this phone," he lied. I didn't realize it at the time, but I'd soon make the same call. And I'd lie as well.

To accommodate his new position at the Pentagon, my father settled us into a split-level, brick rancher in Arlington, Virginia. It was there, at age four, that I finally learned to speak English. Having had my Argentine nanny, Emma, as my primary caregiver during my toddler and preschool years meant I learned and spoke only Spanish, up to that point. The Air Force had stationed my parents in Santiago, Chile, before I was born, and my father picked up Spanish right away, but my mother struggled with the language. Mom, still trying to learn, often had to rely on my father or siblings to translate my chatter to her.

I'm not sure how my mother and I communicated in those

early years. Her broken Spanish made it difficult for her to talk with me, and I gravitated more and more toward Daddy for chatter. He could respond to my endless preschooler questions, although he was unavailable much of the time. My nanny, Emma, served as the surrogate parent I needed.

Once in Arlington, I picked up English pretty quickly, thanks to the two girls next door, Kathy and Tina Flanagan. Although a couple of years older than me, the three of us became the best of friends.

Aside from also being Irish-Catholic, the Flanagan family was as opposite as you might get from ours, and they were quite a spectacle. The father, John, worked as a Coca-Cola distributor. He often reminded my brothers and sister that Pepsi was poison, and they were never to drink it. Trudy, the mom, was a newspaper advice columnist, her guidance loaded with motherhood humor and opinions delivered with unbridled honesty. Trudy never shied away from writing about how haggard she was and how much her appearance reflected this. Her flaming red hair flowed from her head in waves, her long legs striking out of cotton shorts and ending with threadbare thong sandals clinging to her feet. With a baby on one hip, a purse and diaper bag on the other, that was how Trudy moved about most days. With five children ranging from Trish, 17, to the baby, Matt, she was lucky to remember to put on a bra every day.

Living next door, our lives became intertwined, sharing playtime, dinners, and sleepovers — usually at the Flanagan house, not ours, of course. You could find Tina, Kathy and me playing outside every day. Only rain would drive us into a house. The hill behind our houses was perfect for sledding, and we loved playing on it during the deep D.C. snows.

After two years in Arlington, my father was only a few

months away from promotion to General. It must have been tough to pass up such an opportunity, but Argentina called us home. PASA Petroquimica offered him a position he couldn't refuse, so Daddy retired from the Air Force as a full-bird Colonel, and we packed up for another voyage on the Moore-McCormack ocean liner to return to Buenos Aires.

4
OUR HOME IS A CASTLE

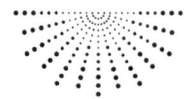

∼

"The world that she lives in is just magical, one of the most beautiful places I've ever seen." - Camilla Belle

∼

The Crisis Center had a steady influx of people coming and going. I gathered a few were just hanging out or meeting up with friends. Others were waiting to see a counselor for some reason or another. I pondered that. *Why were people here? Mostly freaks,* I thought, *but they seem pretty together as a whole.* I sure wasn't, and I feared my presence there, alone on the floor for hours, somehow projected the defeat I felt inside. Desperate to disappear into the block wall, I made myself as small as I could, grabbing my knees close to me and looking down or out the front windows to avoid eye contact. *Stay safe. Stay invisible.* I resumed my ruminations.

I yearned for the familiar sights, sounds, and smells of Argentina that had been absent since we moved back to the United States just two years ago, before tensions with my father reached the next level. The vibrant essence of life in Argentina and the first glimpse of our second home in Buenos Aires flooded my thoughts. I had a vivid recollection from when I was just six years old.

When we drove up, Daddy said, "Nena, this is our new home — a castle just for you!" Our new home was indeed a proper castle, Tudor style and five stories high, with the top floor winding up in a tower turret. The lot covered half of a city block and stayed secured by a six-foot brick and iron fence covered in evergreen shrubs for privacy. Two gated entrances flanked the front, and a smaller iron gate accessed the backyard. A huge stone pergola, about 30 feet long and 12 feet wide, occupied the backyard. It was so well covered in green vines you could sit out in the rain and not get wet. It provided the perfect setting to play school teacher or flight attendant, both of which I enjoyed often.

The suburb of Martinez, where we lived, was an impressive neighborhood with large, elaborate homes. In those days, with no neighborhood gentrification, our lot was sandwiched between two impoverished families and the houses that backed up to them on Avenida Libertador, a main city artery. One of those small houses next to ours belonged to Don Sereno, his wife Antonia, and their daughter Juanita, who was about a year older than me. Don Sereno became our private driver, and once again, the Flynn family enjoyed 24-hour chauffeured transportation.

Don Sereno and his family became a staple in my life. He drove me almost everywhere I went, and he felt like a surrogate uncle. Although he was probably about the same age as our last chauffeur Carlos, they looked nothing alike. The years had been much rougher on Don Sereno, and time had weathered him harshly. His portly figure matched his jovial personality, though, and we loved him for it. I was especially keen to play with his daughter, Juanita. Unfortunately, class structure prevailed, and for reasons I could not understand at all, her father forbade her from going inside our home. She could play with me, but only outside. I struggled to make sense of this ruling and often tried to circumvent it and sneak her into our house, but Juanita was staunchly obedient and never succumbed to my temptations.

Juanita's mom held just as firm and rarely spoke with me. She nodded and smiled when I came through their home. Juanita invited me to her house, but the playdate ended early. I could feel her parents' discomfort with me there, as they ushered us outside to play.

I did, however, finally see inside her home for a few brief minutes. There were no floors, only dirt. Chickens roamed freely between inside and outside the hut. The roof looked like hay and was probably thatch. I'd seen enough to realize the vast contrast between our two homes, yet the differences between us as children were negligible. We just wanted to play with each other.

The other wooden hut abutting our backyard fence housed an elderly woman, most likely in her 80s. The day I met Señora, as I called her, she leaned her frail bony body against the wire fence that stood between our properties, her hands clasping the metal chain links. I approached her and said in Spanish, "I'm Stephanie, and I just moved here." She smiled and nodded in return, and after a few seconds of silence, she finally spoke, "I have lived here in this house all my life." Like Don Sereno's house, hers was a small, thatch-roofed hut, but also with wooden sides and a small front porch where I often saw her in an outdoor straw rocking chair.

The first floor of our home included the sewing room, three maids' bedrooms, kitchen and bath quarters, and a den for us children. Going up to the second floor, our eat-in breakfast room, nestled tightly off the kitchen, afforded me all my meals in the company of the household help — my comfortable family at home. The main formal dining room, shimmering with polished silverware and gleaming crystal glasses, seemed to always be ready for gatherings and dinner parties. In contrast, the smaller formal dining room emitted an intimate ambiance, perfect for the long conversations my parents engaged in every night during their dinner. The living room, next to our elegant entrance, enveloped guests in a sense of refined comfort, with plush sofas and fine art lit up by the streams of light coming through the stained glass windows. The third floor housed our four bedrooms, two baths, and laundry and ironing rooms. This magnificent castle included private patios adjacent to each bedroom. Ascending further to the fourth-floor tower was a hidden treasure — a large walk-in attic space with the requisite eerie feel and musty smell. There was a huge, disturbing painting of Jesus bleeding on the cross propped against the wall. Daddy's sister, my aunt Marjorie, painted it in her macabre, abstract style. I never met Aunt Marjorie. She committed suicide in her 50s, having battled bipolar disorder during a time when medications were not available to ease her torment.

In this majestic home, every floor and every room held its own unique charm. The fifth floor of the tower was a cupola with windows facing all four directions, delivering breathtaking vistas that stretched for miles, revealing the enchanting tapestry of downtown Buenos Aires. As evening fell, the scene transformed into a magical setting. With the city lights shimmering on the eastern horizon, the landscape came alive. A mesmerizing display of sparkling lights danced above the tree lines and Rio de la Plata to our north.

The fourth-floor tower area became my playroom, and while fairly small, it was mostly mine. I had a trunk full of old clothes for dress-up play. My baby doll, named Bobby, and my Barbies and Ken enjoyed a grand two-story home. I built it from cardboard and decorated it with colored pencils, crayons, and bits of fabric scraps that our seamstress, Angela, saved for me. Barbie and Ken had lots of babies, often twins. I loved playing house with them. Barbie was a consummate homemaker and took such loving care of her babies.

I created the most beautiful life for this doll family, with Ken as a hands-on, involved father who loved his wife and children and was never cross with Barbie. "Let's go for a ride to the store," Ken might cheerfully offer. The four of them would go together to the store, a fantasy family playing out scenarios I had never experienced with my human one.

As much as I enjoyed my Barbies, I was just as comfortable outside playing cowboys and Indians, complete with my broomstick horse. The outdoor toolshed, surrounded by boxwood bushes, served as my horse stable. The pergola, with its stone beams and cascading vines, transformed into my countryside cabin home. I even created a small fire pit on the far side of our backyard. These were the sites of countless adventures.

At around seven years old, I let my trusty but imaginary horse, Silver, rest in his stable while I prepared a fire pit to cook hotdogs for dinner. I threw on a couple of extras for my ranch dogs, our German Shepherds Lobo and Gina. In the garage I found a gas can with some fuel in it for the lawn mower. I hauled it all the way back to my fire pit and poured some gas onto a pile of dry sticks I had gathered.

Armed with a pack of matches, also found in the garage, I lit one and couldn't wait for my little fire to burn. It would be so exciting and real. I was surprised when gas that leaked from the can suddenly created a fiery trail to my fire pit. Terrified, I immediately sprang into action, my heart pounding hard. I threw my old wool army blanket over the fire to smother it, and it just fanned the flames further. I finally noticed the garden hose and ran to grab it. At the fence, I saw Señora murmuring just loud enough for me to hear, "Dios mío! Dios mío!" she repeated over and over. I turned the water on and ran to douse the fire. It seemed to work, although the situation remained precarious. As soon as one section of fire went out, another one sprang up. As I continued dousing the fire with the hose, I caught another glimpse of Señora. She looked so frail and scared. I was confident I could keep the fire under control and wondered why she lacked the same assurance. Lobo and Gina paced around nervously but kept strangely quiet.

Eventually I put out the fire, but not before charring the lawn a solid black everywhere the sprinkled drops of gas had landed. Even if I didn't fully understand Señora's fear, I felt guilty for scaring her. I was also worried about the trouble I might face after news of the hazardous episode made its way to my mother. Taborda, our gardener, would likely see the damage and report it back to the maids. They, in turn, would surely tell my mother. To my surprise and relief, no one ever spoke about the backyard fire. I could only surmise that Taborda must have quietly fixed the areas of burned grass without ever telling on me. He was a gem.

Taborda was a handsome man, tall with dark hair and striking facial features, like a model. He often worked as a server at the lavish parties my parents hosted at our home, and he moonlighted as a staff member at the Argentine Presidential Palace.

5
ARGENTINA IS HOME

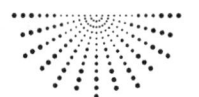

"Home is where one starts from." - T.S. Eliot

I started first grade at the American Community School (ACS), located several miles from our home. The school was a sprawling complex of several traditional and contemporary brick buildings, with the lower elementary grades separated from the middle and high schools. I was fortunate to attend through the seventh grade. The school compound also boasted a variety of recreational spaces. Around the soccer field and baseball diamond, there was an oval track encircling the perimeter of the fields. The track itself had various athletic pads, such as shot put, high jump, and long jump.

Although primarily American students attended the school,

we also had students from the Philippines, Puerto Rico, Singapore, England, Israel, and Venezuela. The first half of our school day was in English, and the second half in Spanish. Most teachers were Argentine or European, with few Americans. Mrs. Passarello, who taught third-grade English was an especially beloved American teacher. I enjoyed my English class so much that year, as Mrs. Passarello impressed upon us the value and importance of honoring our English language by using it well, spelling it correctly, and learning its meanings. Her lifelong lessons served me well.

Our sixth-grade science teacher came from Arkansas and made sure we all knew how to pronounce her state's name properly. Her bleached blonde hair and svelte figure seemed at odds with her otherwise plain appearance. Her choice to wear black clothes every day puzzled us like a cryptic statement that we never deciphered. We didn't connect with her or her lackluster teaching style, and, to our good fortune, she only lasted one semester.

Despite the rare ineffective teacher, ACS offered an excellent education and was a sanctuary for me. I felt a sense of belonging. My teachers and peers liked and appreciated me as I did them, and I relished learning and taking part in sports.

Students and teachers considered me a long-timer since this was my second time living in Argentina and I was fluent in Spanish. Most Americans living in Buenos Aires served one- or two-year stints with various American companies doing business in Argentina. Big names included Esso Oil (later to become Exxon), Goodyear Tires and Dow Chemical. Our second residency in Buenos Aires lasted seven years, long enough to become entrenched in the community and adapt to the split culture of my childhood. Argentina was my home.

I flourished at school. I excelled as an A student and was

naturally athletic, having outgrown my childhood chubbiness. Whether on the field or in the gym during recess and PE, I excelled at archery, pelota-al-cesto (an Argentine form of basketball), gymnastics, soccer, volleyball, and track and field. The one sport I couldn't master was softball. I could never judge the distance between the incoming ball and my hands.

In all my years there, no one ever beat me in running. My best friend, Jackie, came close once during a race in sixth grade for time and team tryouts. I could see Jac next to me as we paced ourselves for the 100 yards. Feeling like I needed to command a larger lead, I sped up, only to find Jackie keeping up with me. When we approached the finish line, I seemed to magically surge forward for the win, but just barely.

My long legs vaulted effortlessly over hurdles. My keen sense of timing allowed me to always make up for lost ground in relays, and I could sail the shot-put puck across the field like a frisbee. The races I found challenging were the 220 and 440. My inner ear ached so badly during those long runs. Sheer determination and an unwavering will propelled me forward, carrying me to the finish line time, and time, again. I had learned to push through physical pain.

Now, crouched on the Crisis Center floor, I couldn't help but wonder if I could push through this inner anguish intensifying by the minute. *Am I going to be okay? What is going to happen to me?* Every question sent a physical reverberation through my body. My athletic and sports life was essentially over — I realized with heavy sorrow. I imagined my school life was over as well. Unfortunately, the excitement of joining the cheerleading squad would not come to fruition.

Whatever faults my father deemed unforgivable, I was sure I possessed a few positive ones. Besides good grades and success in sports, I offered empathy to the new students, seeking newcomers and taking them under my wing, helping them acclimate to our school and life in Argentina. Like my mother, I could always find something I liked about a person, and I believed everyone should accept and care for one another — a lifelong lesson.

On the school bus one day, we picked up two new girls. Nancy was an average-sized girl, but her older sister, Chrissy, was tiny and appeared to suffer from some condition. Chrissy's slight stature was so noticeable that several older boys on the bus lashed out with harsh comments. "You're so little a gust of wind could wipe you out!" and, "What happened to you? Why are you so skinny and small?" I could see Chrissy's eyes welling up with tears. Her sister Nancy sat close but helplessly quiet.

"Stop it!" I yelled at the boys. "Quit teasing her! She can't help how little she is!" I sat behind Chrissy on the bus every day after that to shield her from any further bullying.

Along with empathy, I possessed a rather astute awareness of the feelings of the people around me. On one such occasion, I noticed a student, a grade ahead of me, who had been standing alone every day. He would lean down against the metal railing in front of him and stare out toward the sun with intensity and purpose. The slender boy's look was nondescript, apart from his shock of dark hair and a Jewish Yarmulke bobby pinned to his head.

"Hi, I'm Stephanie," I finally greeted him one day. "I noticed you are new here. Where are you from?" I fully expected a response but was surprised to receive none. He simply stared ahead intently, never uttering a sound. I tried again to reach out to him on another occasion, to no avail. I often wondered what secrets burdened him.

My share of bullying still lay ahead of me, but as a young girl, I felt deeply protective of my friends.

6
MI PAPO

"To the world you are a dad. To our family, you are the world."
- Author Unknown

I was Gordon Flynn's darling, and he was my hero, no doubt. I thought he was the smartest man who ever lived, so mentally strong and brave. When I was 6 years old, my father taught me to play the card game gin, and I became good at it. We kept a running score going for several years, and I actually surpassed my father's score on several occasions. My skills impressed him, and he loved having a worthy challenger. Our gin games became a daily ritual after his workday and evening nap. Our special time together always included snuggling on his bed, where he shared stories about his family and WWII, but most often, stories about his beloved mother,

Marjorie. He worshiped her. As an adult, I would learn that she died in her 50s from breast cancer. I never had the chance to meet her. My mother once told me that my grandmother had confided in her about finding a lump on her breast. My mother tried in vain to get her to see a doctor. Marjorie was too embarrassed to have her breasts examined, even by a physician, and refused to go.

Although I never met her, I at least felt acquainted with her. My father made sure I knew how perfect she was. A slim woman with dark curls draped softly over her shoulders, she was a beauty to behold. Her striking features and soft eyes drew attention from both men and women in her presence. She often hosted card parties, smoked cigarettes, and, despite prohibition, served her illegally brewed beer. She entertained guests with her talents for singing and playing the piano, and the poker games often continued long into the night. Rather than condemn her, my father lauded any questionable behavior as endearing mischief. His mother was flawless in his eyes and could do no wrong.

Daddy also loved our casino fantasy, telling it over and over. "Nena," he would exclaim, "we will take three pennies to a casino on the Riviera and win millions with it! Then we will use those millions to live lavishly by the sea in Barcelona, Spain." The story grew year after year, dramatically embellished, but the basic premise remained the same. I often fantasized about living with our millions. The Riviera sounded enchanting, and the thought of living by a beach in a Mediterranean setting enthralled me.

My father loved to tease me, too. He would walk around his room with a funny gait, kicking his heels up behind him. "Nena, I'm going to walk you down the wedding aisle like this!" he would say with a sly grin.

"No, papo, no! You can't do that!" I pled, mortified.

All of his teasing eventually caught on with me. One evening, he lay in bed and I sat on his chest. Looking him in the face, I asked cheekily, "Hey, papo, do you want a Kranger, yes or no?"

"Well," he answered cautiously, "What is a Kranger?"

"I can't tell you that. You have to answer yes or no and then I can tell you." I grinned nervously, not quite sure what his response would be. I hoped for a yes from him. After considering his options for a moment, he finally answered, "Yes! Give me a Kranger."

Before he could change his mind, I quickly raised my right arm and punched my father squarely in his left eye. It was a moment I couldn't quite believe was actually happening. More like an out-of-body experience, it felt like watching someone else do it. *Surely I hadn't just punched my father in the eye?* But I had. I socked him right in his eye with the might of a 6-year-old. Somehow I was still there — breathing, alive, and capable of thinking about it.

My father stayed calm and finally said, "Well, I did ask for one." Relief swept through me. "That's what I get for being a gambling man," he concluded.

My father also had a ritual of telling me to lie on my back on his bed while he grabbed my ankles and pulled on my legs. According to him, this would lengthen my legs and make me taller. Daddy felt you could never be too tall, too thin, or too rich.

To my father, being fluent in three languages was much better than two. Despite no interest on my part, he had my mother enroll me in private French lessons when I was 10 years old. I would walk or ride my bike several blocks to a tutor's house for lessons. I found the sessions boring, but I enjoyed the praise from my father when I came home and regurgitated the phrases I had learned that day. Private piano lessons and, later, guitar followed. I did not become proficient in any of these pursuits, though I had asked for the guitar lessons. I loved my young teenage teacher. She taught me standards like 'House of the Rising Sun' and 'Jamaica Farewell.' When she moved to Switzerland for college, I had no desire to find another teacher. I couldn't imagine anyone ever measuring up to her and the bond we had formed.

Daddy seemed patient with my various extracurricular activities and their uninspired results. He didn't have that level of tolerance for all my endeavors and antics.

7
IL CAPO

~

"An unpredictable parent is a fearsome god in the eyes of a child." - Susan Forward

~

"For Pete's sake, Louise!" I heard the phrase almost daily for as long as I could remember. It overflowed with disdain. My father was forever belittling my mom with painful regularity. She always owned up to whatever accusation he spouted at her, and I cringed inside. The questions began circulating in my head when I was far too young to contemplate such adult ideas. *Why does he have to talk to her with such disrespect?* I loved my mom, and I thought he did, too. *"Why would he treat her that way if he loves her? Why do they sleep in separate, single beds? Why doesn't he treat her like he treats me? Why does she put up with it?"*

I could hear him lambasting my mother through their closed bedroom doors. "Why on earth would you let her cut her hair like that?" he fumed. I thought it was a fun idea to take a pair of scissors to my head at age seven. Before she could explain she didn't realize I had been cutting my hair, he continued the verbal assault. "How does she find scissors to do such a thing? Why aren't you monitoring her more closely, Louise?" On and on he went, each assertion more condescending than the last. I felt horrible — ashamed and guilty. He liked my hair to be long with short bangs. Deviating from that was not an option, and evidently, it fell under mother's responsibility. My father called the shots in our house and my mother's role was to keep order and implement the discipline on us children. She was relegated to bad cop even though, in reality, he doled out both the laws and sentencing.

He often brought home chi-ches, little gifts, on his way home from work, usually new binchas, soft stretchy headbands purchased from street vendors' carts. Binchas represented a win-win for him. I delighted in getting a chi-che, and if worn properly, the bincha would help flatten my large ears to my head in time. Or so he hoped. Flat ears and long legs.

When my father came home to find me with a rag, dusting the long mahogany staircase banister that led to our upstairs bedrooms, he entered their room, furiously reprimanding my mother for allowing me to dust like a housekeeper. "Why is Stephanie out there with rags in her hands cleaning like a maid?!" he yelled incredulously. Like the haircut incident, my mother did not know I had been outside their room "cleaning." Before she could stammer out a response, he berated, "You shouldn't let her do these things, Louise! What is wrong with you? I don't want her ever doing maid's work!"

I didn't understand what was so wrong. *What could possibly be so awful? It was fun pretending to clean my house*, I thought. I didn't understand that I once again bumped up against classism and overstepped the boundaries of my class. Like so many times before and since, I was once again weighed down with guilt for unintentionally getting my mother in trouble with my father for something she played no part in. In my father's eyes, only my mother was to blame. I never seemed at fault. It made little sense to me. Even then, as a small child, I knew these reprimands my mother received for deeds of mine only fed her growing resentment toward me. I sensed my mother envied my relationship with my father. He gave me the attention she craved.

It must've been a harsh smart ass comment the day I talked back to my mom. Though I can't even remember what I said to her, before the words were completely out of my mouth, my mother slapped me across the face. I was stunned. It was so uncharacteristic of her to lash out. She had never laid a hand on me — ever, that I could remember.

I felt in my gut that it was my father who she actually wanted to slap. Retreating to my room, feeling caught in the middle once again, I cried softly into my pillow. I never wanted to hurt my mom enough to make her want to slap me. She later apologized to me, saying she was worn out and had overreacted, but her words rang hollow. "I'm sorry," I muttered in return, still feeling guilty for angering her.

8
MY FAMILY

"Excellence is not an exception; it is a prevailing attitude."
- Colin Powell

My mother wasn't especially hands on or particularly involved in my life, but she was my mother, and I loved her. On some level, I knew she loved me, too.

A remarkable woman, my mother earned her pilot's license at a mere 20 years old, having learned how to fly as a teenager. When World War II broke out, she became a pilot in the highly competitive WASP (Women Airforce Service Pilots) program. The WASP, founded by Jaqueline Cochran, a friend of Amelia Earhart, piloted airplanes, ferrying military men and aircraft across the country from one base to another, testing new airplanes, or transporting planes from one location to another. My parents met as fellow pilots and married soon after at Roswell Air Force Base in New Mexico. Far from the adventurous life she once led, her existence now revolved around taking care of our house, the servants, and my father. Everything started and ended with pleasing my father. Keeping Daddy happy was not a simple task, and my mother was mentally exhausted from the constant effort. Her nightly cocktail hour with my father was her treasured respite. She overimbibed most nights, resulting in squinting, blinking eyes along with unnatural mouth movements. Beverage hour was also the time when she was most likely to express her love for me.

My mother delegated most of my basic care to the maids, primarily Alberta, one of our live-in servants. She was the person with whom I ate all my meals, who accompanied me to town, and who cared for my daily needs. For all practical purposes, she was a surrogate mom or sister, and she meant the world to me. She was only 15 when she came to work for us, and she was the only servant who stayed the full seven years we lived in Buenos Aires this time around. I can't imagine my life without her. On the few occasions when I could attend a movie, Alberta took me. Shopping for shoes? Alberta went with me. Going to visit her family at the other end of the city? Yes, she would take me. I felt as much a part of her family as she was of mine. She was my confidante, my sounding board, and my encourager. She held my hand everywhere we went, making me feel close and connected to someone important in my life, feeling cared for.

We ate dinner in our formal dining room as a family once a month. On those evenings, Alberta, dressed in her formal black uniform and starched white apron, served our meals. She quietly moved from person to person, approaching on our left to offer us food from sterling silver platters. I felt uncomfortable and embarrassed being served by her. We never made eye contact during those dinners, preferring to avoid our awkward discomfort.

We were used to sharing our meals together at the kitchen table with all the household help. There would be table wine passed around amongst them and lively talks about their families and politics, particularly their love of Juan Peron and disdain for Evita, his wife.

Alberta and my parents were major influences during my childhood. I adored my three older siblings, too, but they only played a small part in my childhood memories. By the time I was eight and nine, they had all left for the States to attend college and the Air Force Academy. Gordy would follow in both of my parents' footsteps and become a pilot. The twins, Henry and Ivette, both went to college at my father's alma mater, the University of Georgia in Athens.

My eldest sister, Laura, was 25 and a mother to two girls when I was born, so we never lived in a household together. She was my mother's child from a young first marriage, a truth we understood never to discuss. I visited Laura in the U.S. every July, staying with her and my nieces in Atlanta, Georgia. They kept a houseboat at nearby Lake Lanier, where we stayed for a few weeks each year. By we, I mean me. I traveled alone to my sister's house, not knowing where my parents would go while I was there. My nieces and later an adopted nephew were close to my age. Josephine, the third and youngest daughter, was only a week younger than me. Though we lived polar-opposite lives, we were best buds. She was the skinny, cute, horse-loving one, and I was the chubby, dog-loving, brainy one.

I learned early on to embrace being the brainy one. My father expressed great pride with every good report card.

Excelling in academics, intelligence, perfection, and financial wealth surpassed all other accomplishments. As much as my father valued scholastic achievement, my parents never attended school or sporting events. They avoided any involvement, so I rode to functions with friends and their parents. I didn't object. I was keenly aware my parents were a lot older than my friends' parents. They were both 41 years old when I was born, and their age was a source of embarrassment for me when, at the tender 'tween stage, I wanted nothing more than to fit in and be just like everyone else. Everyone else had young, vibrant, good-looking, happily involved parents. Mine? They looked old enough to be grandparents, probably because they were. They didn't harbor any interest in school track meets or events. I vowed when I grew up and had children, I would be young, vibrant, and involved, and I'd look the best that I could — like Mary Wilton's mom. She was so beautiful and elegant with her long thick hair wrapped into a neat French twist, and her long polished nails and perfect makeup.

I couldn't even fathom my father attending a picnic or sitting on the bleachers at a sporting event. It was beneath him, I thought, to attend school events with common folks. Golfing was as casual as my father got. He didn't own a pair of corduroys, much less jeans. My father reserved his presence for business, galas, or golfing. He limited his time with us children to occasional formal dinners at home and a twice a year outing to an upscale restaurant. These dinners always served up impeccable table manners as a first course.

The colonel ran a strict household. He instilled in my siblings, as he did with me, the importance of academic excellence. Intelligence and perfection. I didn't know what would happen if you failed to meet his silent demands, and I never intended to find out. Daddy's expectations stretched beyond what seemed reasonable at any age, and the mundane and inane were not excluded from his endless requirements of us.

"Never walk with your feet pointing out like a duck, Nena. Your mother and sister look awful walking around like ducks. Keep your feet straight when you walk. Remember that," he added for emphasis.

"Always be on time Nena. Do not be late for anything! Your mother and sister are always late. It is slovenly and disrespectful to be late," he advised as I sat next to him, both relieved and thrilled to be ready and waiting with him for us to go to dinner as a family. *No, sir, he will never have to talk down to or about me. I will always be perfect for Daddy*, I thought to myself. Unbeknownst to me, the weight of his disappointment would one day engulf me.

9
APPEARANCES

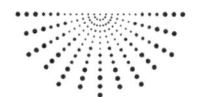

"We are prisoners of our own experience."
- Edward R. Murrow

Few friends ever met my father. If Daddy was home, we were relegated outdoors. Luckily, he spent every Saturday and Sunday at the golf course. I felt guilty that sleepovers only took place at friends' houses, rarely at my house in return. I could only have a friend spend the night when my father was out of town on a weekend night. He preferred not to have his routine disrupted by the noise of children playing.

I had only one sleepover party during my childhood, in fifth grade, when I was 11. My father was in Boston attending Harvard Business School for several months, and my mother had facelift surgery while he was gone. He'd often criticize her down-turned mouth, saying it made her look like she was always frowning. He suggested she keep a perpetual smile on her face to mask any signs of discontent or aging. Although pleased she had taken his suggestion to get a facelift, he wanted it done during his absence so the procedure would not interfere with his daily life. Any neglect he would have to endure for the time it would take her to recover from a major surgery was unacceptable. And he didn't want to see her in stitches, all swollen, bruised, and unattractive.

My mother must have planned for a lot of things to get done while my father was gone to the U.S. It's the only reason I can imagine that she would have arranged for my one and only sleepover to take place on the day of her surgery.

I was so excited to finally be hosting friends at home that I pushed aside any worry about the fact that our living room was far from conducive to a tween party. Marble floors draped with a fine Persian rug, pearl-white satin sofas, a baby grand piano and original oil paintings — one with naked cherubs all over it and another of an exposed woman breastfeeding a baby. I felt really awkward and embarrassed looking at those paintings. It didn't seem right to be showing private parts so freely and openly, even if some were only cherubs.

I was determined to make the best of the situation and did what I could to ensure my friends had a good time. We engaged in the requisite liquor cabinet inspection and tasting. We played games, giggled, laughed, and had great fun. Until 10 p.m. That's when my mother leaned over the staircase banister and announced to my girlfriends that she had just endured facelift surgery in the morning and couldn't tolerate the noise. I died inside. At my friends' homes, their parents engaged with us most of the time and by no means told us to quiet down during sleepovers. I felt sick inside. My only sleepover was certain to be judged a flop. The following week at school, I imagined whispers of the ill-fated sleepover. I stuffed the insecure feelings away.

My father's strict, demanding perfectionism rubbed off on me unwittingly. I learned at a young age that appearances were everything. How the world sees you is of crucial importance, and you must maintain your image at all costs. We were never to talk about personal family issues with each other or anyone else. It was just understood.

We children couldn't even journal. I once received a diary from a relative at Christmas when I was 11, but it never made it to my bedroom. It was likely re-gifted to someone by my mother. I never asked about it. If you couldn't talk about family issues, I damn sure knew not to write them down. Although I couldn't remember who gave me the diary, I often fantasized that it must have been my great Aunt Agnes Stephanie — the writer who published columns in The Atlanta Journal and Constitution and my namesake. It seemed so fitting.

10
THE DARKER SIDES

"The threat of violence can be almost as stressful as actually suffering or witnessing violence." - L. Eugene Arnold

By fifth or sixth grade, I could take the colectivos, city buses, by myself, and walk to the station to ride the trains on my own. I wondered if my mom realized what she was doing, letting me out on the streets so much. Even at six and seven, I walked everywhere in our neighborhood.

At 11 or 12 years old, my friends and I walked or rode our bikes to the pizza parlor by the train station and ordered deep dish meat pizzas, a pure delicacy for me, as pizza went against Daddy's strict dietary rules for the family. No fried foods, no potatoes, no pasta, no corn or starchy vegetables, no bread with dinner, and certainly no pizza. Because Daddy loved it, he allowed white rice.

The ice cream store at the gas station a block away from our house became a daily stop for me on my way home from school once I started taking the colectivos home instead of the school bus. I ordered ice cream or alfajores, a powdered sugar-coated cookie filled with dulce-de-leche, a favorite of mine.

Riding bikes to different friends' homes gave me a much-loved sense of freedom. Most often I would ride to Melissa's or, after she moved back to the States, Scott's house. Playing basketball outside along with Ralphie and others who might drop by became a daily ritual after school. Scott, who was my best friend from first grade on, became my first boyfriend in sixth grade and gave me my first kiss. I felt a strong connection with him and relished our time together as friends and then as a pre-teen couple.

I became somewhat street smart at an early age, seeing and experiencing more than a child should. Coming across men jerking off in their cars and leaving the door open to make sure you saw them stroking their fleshy members became normalized because I had nothing else for comparison.

This happened at least a dozen times over the years, starting as early as 7 years old. Sometimes it wasn't just shocking, it was scary. Men enjoyed chasing me down the street in their cars, so I learned to outmaneuver them. Walking once with some newbie friends, we came across one of those perverts. As soon as I saw the passenger door open, I knew what we were going to encounter, but it was too late. Walking ahead of me, my friend Sheryl suddenly let out a piercing scream that echoed through the air. Her body froze in place, her eyes fixated on the sight before us — a massive, sturdy brown penis, standing firm for our viewing. I grabbed her and Melissa's arms and started running. Sure enough, he reacted like a predatory animal. I knew he'd have to take the time to close his car door and turn around, so I pulled my friends in the opposite direction to gain a bigger head start. Sheryl was screaming as he chased us, and I couldn't get her to stop. We took a sharp left and disappeared into Sheryl's backyard to lose him.

Anonymity was the most essential maneuver. Don't let them see which house you go into, or they will come back to harass you. I learned this the hard way when a stalker chased me and saw me run through our backyard gate. After that, he parked beside our property and waited for me to go into the backyard to the swimming pool, then masturbated through the iron gate, staring at me the whole while. I didn't know what to make of it. I didn't even know what he was doing. But I knew it was gross and creeped me out. And I knew it scared me.

I finally told Alberta about it. She, in turn, told my mom, which earned me a little sit-down chat with my mother. "Stephanie, Alberta tells me that a man has been coming to the backyard gate and bothering you." I nodded in silence, too embarrassed to talk about it. "If he comes back," she continued, "let me or Alberta know." I don't recall mentioning the visits to anyone again, so he must have eventually stopped. But there were many additional confrontations with deviants on the streets, some showing off their sexual organs. As much as these encounters unnerved me, I didn't let them stop me from participating in life. They did make me consistently aware of my surroundings, prompting my innate intuition to thrive. I also became more desensitized as the obnoxious occurrences repeated themselves.

We lived three blocks from Rio de la Plata, a large estuary formed from the merging of the Paraná and the Uruguay rivers, coming through South America via Brazil and Uruguay, past

Buenos Aires, and flowing into the Atlantic Ocean. My friends and I loved to go down to the river and roam around the woods and water. We once found a cow upside down and dead — all chewed up. One of the locals told us piranhas had gotten to it during high tide. Aside from piranhas and tides, the real danger to us was the local bums and winos who hung around the river's edge. We entered the river area through a community park, where there were a lot of poor people milling about from the stilted shacks along the river's border. We all maintained a sense of harmony by avoiding each other and minding our own business.

During a visit to the river's edge, a 20-something Argentine guy in a truck decided to teach us a lesson. He didn't like rich American kids, and he wanted us to know it, yelling at us as he chased us into the river with his truck. "You rich American kids are rotten! Pieces of shit!" he hollered in Spanish. Once again, I tried to calm my friends as we fled deeper and deeper into the water to avoid getting hit or, worse, run over by this madman's truck.

The undercurrents strengthened, and I knew we couldn't go much further for risk of being swept away, while the tall wheels of the truck seemed to drive through any depth of water. Up past our waists and fully clothed, we ran further into the river to save ourselves. Each time we tried to slog back toward shore, he revved his engine and charged toward us, laughing through his muddy windshield, enjoying his intimidation. "You are stupid Americans, you are!!!" he howled. We were terrified, with no idea how to escape our dangerous predicament. After 30 minutes of torment, fighting the river current and our aggressor, we were exhausted. We surveyed our surroundings, and with one last surge of adrenaline, we swam to the outside rim, scrambling up a concrete wall. We barely made it, and no sooner than our feet reached the top of the wall, he pounded his truck against it.

He had every intention of smashing us into the wall with that truck. We dropped over the side of the wall and ran full tilt to my friend Melissa's house, since she lived closest to the river. As always, we kept the harrowing episode to ourselves, fearing that our parents would take away our freedoms if they learned about the dangers we encountered on the streets.

The rear of our school and the adjacent sports field backed up to train tracks and Rio de la Plata. Along the riverbanks, between the railroad tracks and the river, were dozens of shacks up on stilts, overflowing with large, impoverished families. I often found myself staring at their homes and contemplating the difficulties of their lives. The older I got, the more aware I became they were peaceful, hardworking, but despairing people. Most families had more children than they could care for and just as many elders to look after. I imagined it to be a miserable existence and pitied them. Once in a while, when I'd wave and say "Hi," one of them would wave back. Would a smile and a wave make any difference? I remember hoping so.

During fourth grade, we once had a competitive soccer game going on in the far corner of the massive schoolyard during recess. Above the noisy screams and jabbering we heard yelling from the railroad tracks. As we glanced toward the voices, two drunk men in their 30s or 40s, dressed in stained rags, firmly grasped wine bottles as they swayed on the tracks. We quickly gathered against the 20-foot-high chain-link fence, hanging our hands in the metal links as we listened to one man yell to us in slurred Spanish, "You violent Americans! This is what you evil Americans do in Vietnam. You murder people in Vietnam!" We watched, horrified, as he slammed his drunk buddy onto the tracks, placing his head on one of the train rails. Then he raised a leg and, with all the drunk force he could muster, slammed his boot on the side of his friend's head. The injured man screamed out in pain. The man raised his leg and smashed his friend's head again. And again, railing about violent Americans. "You are evil people, you Americans! You kill innocent people!"

I can't recall how many times he struck, but it was gut-wrenching to watch. I barely comprehended all his rantings about depraved Americans, unable to take my focus off the bloodied man now lying motionless on the tracks. His friend's head had been smashed out of shape, and blood was seeping from it. He lay there on the tracks, silent, bloodied, and still.

By this time, the teachers on the field had reached us and physically pulled us off the fence. Some students were frozen to the chain link, locked in terror and shock by what we had just witnessed. Although the teachers yanked us away, it didn't stop us from running to the side fence where a police car had finally pulled up. The two officers took their time getting out of the car and casually strolling up to the drunk man, who still stood on the tracks. Several of us students started yelling to the police, "The wino you are talking to attacked the man beat up on the tracks. That's the guy who is guilty! Take him away and lock him up!" They ignored our cries. We couldn't hear what they said, but we could see what had transpired.

The police officers motioned to the drunk to go on his way while one of them dragged the victim's body from the tracks, through the dirt and across the sidewalk, stuffing him into the back seat of the police car. He looked dead. We witnessed the police allowing a maniacal monster to walk away while they let a murderer go free. This obvious and horrific injustice affected me irrevocably. It left me cold.

11
THE GLASS FAMILY

"That still feels like the most accurate description — I felt homesick, but I was home." - Sarah Silverman

When I was around ten, my parents planned a vacation to North Africa and Europe. My father easily arranged a month-long vacation without me, as he was never one to let children interfere with his ambitions. They offered to rent our house to a family who were new to Buenos Aires and needed a temporary place to stay while they searched for a home. One caveat. The rental of our home would come with me in it. Unbelievable as it seemed, my parents left me in our house, with a whole new cast of characters residing in the other bedrooms.

I met the Glass family — my new roommates and guardians

— on the day they moved in. Mrs. Glass was a tall, ample woman who appeared to be in her mid-to late 30s. Animated, unrestrained, and affable, her persona enthralled me. Mr. Glass balanced his wife, exuding a calmer, slightly more reserved manner, with an amusing sense of humor. He had a stocky build and rough, aging features topped with salt and pepper hair that was both receding and unruly.

Their teenage daughter, Linda, was a thin, spunky, pretty girl with thick brown hair. It was cut into a popular bob with the ends tucked under ever so slightly. They all seemed like nice enough people, but I soon realized I could not make any sense around the idea of strangers sitting on my parents' chairs, sleeping in their beds — they pushed the two single beds together — and occupying their spots at the dining room table. Despite attempting to adapt, I couldn't adjust to this new family living in our home. I was depressed and feigned sickness in order to stay home from school. I would lie in my bed and write letter after letter to my parents, asking them to please come home. After a week, I realized my parents would not be coming home. I locked away the feelings of sadness the best I could and pressed on. Back to school I went, and life somehow carried on. But not without a nagging feeling of aloneness shadowing me. I felt dispensable, a foreshadowing of how disposable I would one day become.

The Glass family treated me well, and despite my intense sadness, I could accept and appreciate their kindness.

One evening, Mr. Glass heard me playing school in the hallway outside of my bedroom, which was right next to my parents' room. "Stephanie," he called out to me, "why don't you come in here for just a minute, please." Clad in my doll's long nightgown I transformed into a dress, I attempted to imitate Señorita Christina's signature style of short dresses. I thought her dresses were so pretty and she attractive in them — snug-fitting short dresses and skirts always paired up with pointed-toe stiletto heels. Along with her waist-length, flowing blonde hair, Señorita Christina, one of our Spanish teachers, looked so fashionable. Always. My doll's nightgown landed on my thighs, and I borrowed high heels to wear from Mother's shoe closet. I entered their room with a mischievous grin. Mr. Glass smiled widely and said, "I hear you playing school and you are such a wonderful teacher, Stephanie! Your students must love you!"

I grinned meekly and replied, "Thank you."

"Put your legs together Stephanie, I want to see something," he requested, and I complied. "Look at that!" he suddenly exclaimed. "You have perfect legs! They make three diamonds when you press them together. That is the sign of ideal shaped legs!"

After grinning and thanking him again, I returned to playing school in the hallway, feeling a newfound pride in my well-shaped legs as I walked confidently, in high-heeled shoes, between the chairs I had lined up for my students' seats.

Mrs. Glass always made it a point to talk to me after school, much like my mom on the days she was home. "How was your day at school, Stephanie?" she inquired. "Did you have fun at recess? What was your yummy lunch today?" The questions continued. I answered politely and with little fanfare.

Living with the Glass family provided me with the opportunity to observe their family dynamics firsthand. They seemed the polar opposite of us, and it was the first time I realized how different our family might actually be. I had seen the differences between my friends' families and ours, but the contrast didn't affect me as greatly as living with the Glass family did.

They were mellow, pleasant people. They didn't argue that I could hear. In fact, they laughed a lot. They seemed to truly enjoy their meals together as a family, with engaging and enthusiastic conversations.

Their daughter Linda was very kind to me. She often took me out with her as she visited friends nearby or shopped along Avenida Libertador, a block away from our home. On one occasion, Linda took me to her good friend's house, Veronica, who also lived in a multi-storied, gray stone castle.

The family's butler let us in and went to retrieve Veronica upstairs. As we waited in the front marbled foyer, I gazed around the opulent home showcasing priceless antiques and baubles collected around the world. I loved how spacious, airy, and bright it was. Although the family was American, they moved to Argentina from London, England, where they had lived since Veronica was a toddler. As I heard footsteps on the marble curved staircase, I turned to discover what I was sure was a live angel. Veronica was wearing a long white nightgown with a matching robe — both made of indulgent silk and trimmed with fine white fur. Her house shoes were delicate satin slippers with pointed toes, kitten heels, and a tuft of fur on top. Her long blonde locks draped over her furry shoulders like a cosmic hug. As soon as she spoke to us in her luscious English accent, I was smitten. She descended the stairs like a princess, and in my mind, that was exactly what she was. A stunning princess. Linda, by comparison, was very down to earth, and I appreciated her so much as well. I learned about grace, pleasant manners, kindness, and beauty. The day spent with the teenagers, their joyous laughter, and bright smiles, remains a treasured memory, deeply etched into my mind.

A few weeks after the Glass family moved out of our house and my parents returned from their African and European adventure, my mother said Mrs. Glass called and wanted me to come out and visit them at their new home for a luncheon they were hosting. Surprised and honored that they missed me, I wanted to see them again.

The outdoor luncheon boasted long cloth-covered tables, arranged flowers, and a stunning tablescape. Sitting among their vast group of friends, I felt proud and happy to know such an exceptional family. Most memorable from that special day was being served iced coffee for the first time. I knew from then on that I loved everything about coffee. Milk and sugar made the flavor combination even richer.

12
HONORS AND HONESTY

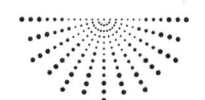

"Between stimulus and response, there is a space. In that space is our power to choose our response. In our response lies our growth and our freedom." - Vicktor Emil Frankl

A big turning point in my life came in mid-1968, when I was 12. My favorite teacher pulled me aside one day to let me know I had the highest grade point average in the whole sixth-grade. The reward for this academic achievement was being appointed the carrier of the American flag for all school auditorium events during our seventh-grade year. One of my best friends, Mary Wilton, got the second highest GPA and would carry the Argentine flag next to me. I was stunned. I didn't know that they tracked grades, let alone selected our flag carriers based on that. The thought of my father's excitement thrilled me, and I couldn't wait to share the announcement when I got home. He was ecstatic upon hearing the auspicious news.

When the day finally arrived that I would carry the flag down the red carpet of our school auditorium for the first time, the sight of my parents in the audience startled me. They showed no interest in school functions, and they had not mentioned attending the ceremony. I cringed at the sight of them sitting in the back row. My carefully guarded secret about my older parents was now out.

I was both nervous and in awe over my first trip down the aisle as it was. Mary and I carried our respective flags down the two auditorium aisles, standing up straight with pride and a respectable amount of reverence. We managed our maiden performance flawlessly and felt so honored.

After the event, my parents met me in the school lobby where I busied myself, putting away the flag and avoiding eye contact. Mortified, I didn't know how to respond or react. Most of my friends had never met my father, and I had never been seen at school with my parents. I tried to sound casual, asking my parents how long they planned to stay. Not one to miss a hidden agenda or let it slide, my father pressed to know why I wanted to know. I didn't want to lie, but lacked the finesse of diplomacy, and answered bluntly, muttering, "I don't want my friends to see how old my parents are." As if the world were moving in slow motion, I heard the words come out of my mouth one by one. Shame overcame me as I spoke, and I hung my head as I broke out in a nervous sweat. My father didn't say a word. He turned silently on his heel and headed out the front door of the school, my mother in tow.

That was it.

I had worked so hard my whole life to never cross that

dreaded line with my father, and in one sentence I managed to not only cross the line but barrel past it, landing hard on the other side with an epic crash. My father's considerable ego couldn't tolerate such an impudent statement from a preteen.

That was a pivotal moment. One that began the eventual destruction of my relationship with my father. A scholastic honor that should've become a cherished memory instead set events in motion, inevitably contributing to my abandonment at the crisis center.

I shifted on the floor, pained by the stark realization and connection. Images and emotions from the fallout came flooding back.

Daddy had refused to speak to me for several weeks. Each day I was met with dead silence, no recognition other than an occasional nod of his head. I was crushed. One day, I summoned the courage to ask my mom why Daddy was no longer speaking to me. She confirmed my fears. He'd taken offense to what I said that day at the school assembly. Intuitively, I already knew, but I needed to hear her say it. I ran the scenario over in my mind endlessly for months. *Why would I say such a thing? Why was I so horrible? Why did I care so much about appearances? How selfish of me to put my ridiculous feelings before those of my father.*

No more gin games in the evenings, no more stories, no chiches, no more excitement about greeting Daddy with good news. One sentence decimated all of it. Even though I apologized to him at my mother's suggestion, his feelings toward me were lukewarm from that day forward. He taught me, alright. His outright rejection damaged my psyche irreparably and altered my life path.

As much as I missed my father, I knew nothing I could do would repair our relationship. No number of apologies or cajoling would move him. Despite losing much of my motivation for good grades, I persevered and continued living my life. I excelled in sports, especially track and field. It was my most gratifying outlet, affording me necessary challenges and goals.

Coincidentally, at the same time, our physical education coach revealed that our school had been invited to a significant summer intramural track and field meet in Brazil. She tapped me for the team that would represent our school. My best friend Jackie also made the team, so I was thrilled. We were so proud and excited to participate, compete, and travel. We increased our training and worked hard for the coming track meet. This meant extra hours of training after school on most days.

13
DEVASTATION

"Grief is love's unwillingness to let go." - Unknown

In May 1969, my parents revealed we would move to Atlanta, Georgia, in July. I was instantly grief stricken. I begged and pleaded for them to leave me with a family in Buenos Aires. American dependents often remained for a school year or several years if their parents transferred elsewhere or returned to the U.S. I was sure I could find one of my friends' families to take me in, but my parents wouldn't hear of it. The same parents who left me with virtual strangers for a vacation now wouldn't even consider allowing me to stay with friends during the school year. I was finally mature enough to handle it, and I probably could've lived with the Glass family, for one. They grew fond of me while renting our house, and I believe they'd have gladly housed me.

But no, we were leaving. For good. The sight of packed suitcases, stacks of boxes and empty rooms filled the space with a sense of finality. The deafening silence echoed through the house, as if the walls themselves mourned our impending departure. As I walked through the box-lined hallways, the absence of chatter was palpable, leaving a hollow feeling in my chest. The weight of leaving behind my friends, my beloved school, and the familiar faces of my caring teachers pressed down on me with a looming dread. Even my loyal dogs and Alberta, my constant companions, seemed to sense the impending loss. I shuffled around the various rooms, gathering as many memories as my young mind could hold and filing them into my heart. A wave of devastation washed over me as I faced the reality of bidding farewell to everything I had ever known and loved.

Moving a continent away also meant we had to purge our belongings. We would be living in a small apartment with no room for the voluminous possessions occupying our five-story home. I came home from school one day to find an estate sale in full force and watched in despair as everything that represented home was sold off. I felt especially crushed when I discovered that someone had bought my baby doll, Bobby. My one baby doll, whom I had taken such good care of, had been sold off to a fate unknown. Same with Barbie and her perfect family. All of them gone — Barbie, Ken, their babies, and the car. Someone tossed their lovingly crafted cardboard dream house in the trash.

Having lived vicariously through them for so long, I was shattered. The sudden sale and move to parts unknown of my pretend, happy families mirrored the disintegration and skewed trajectory of my life. Someone threw out all my dress-up clothes, too. In fact, no toys remained at all. It didn't matter to me I was 13 and too old to play with them; they still held sentimental value to me. I had earned most of the money to buy them, mainly through good grades at school. They all represented an important part of me. Thankfully, nobody had sold my 45s and LPs. I could keep those, along with my desktop record player and guitar.

My best friend Jackie gave me a going-away party. While we played hide and seek during the party, I hid myself under a small table, covered with a ruffled cloth, and tears soon flowed down my cheeks. The people, school, and country I loved made leaving unbearable. My parents' decision to move us away from the only home I'd ever known and loved made me angry. That my father barely spoke to me was vapid. I didn't care to speak to him anymore, either. As far as I was concerned, he was ripping my life to shreds.

The day we left Argentina, I sat in the back seat of our car between my parents, as Don Sereno drove us one last time in our Chevy Impala, now bequeathed to him. I looked up at the front door landing of the castle to see Alberta, by then 22 years old, standing with our two German shepherds, Jet and Gina. Alberta waved a slow queen's wave goodbye to us. I leaned forward to catch a last glimpse of her and slowly waved back, suppressing the overwhelming urge to let out mournful sobs as unruly tears spilled down my face. My cherished Alberta ... *how could I leave her? How could I leave my beloved dogs? What would happen to them? Were they going to a new home? Would they be put down?* Endless aching questions with no answers and a deep, echoing despondency trapped me in deep sadness.

14
LIFE IN ATLANTA

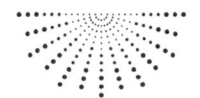

"We learn flexibility and adaptability." - John Roper

No glamorous ocean liner awaited us this time. In July, we flew unceremoniously back to the U.S., landing in Miami. My father arranged for us to stay for a few days in Miami Beach, which had a long commercial strip lit up from one end to the other. It reminded me of the Brazilian beaches I had relished visiting as a child. Light winds carried with them the alluring hint of sand and salt, dusting passersby with ocean mist. Neon signs lined the sidewalks, their bright colors flashing like warning signs. Along the waterline, the bright moon shone explosively across the oceanfront, the waves moving its glow like dancers on the surface. As beautiful as it was, my mood remained unchanged, dejected, and defeated.

Our high-rise hotel had a ballroom, and one night after we dined to the sounds of a big band playing, Daddy took Mother to the dance floor for a spin. I was thoroughly embarrassed. I had rarely seen my father hug, kiss, or show any affection to my mother. Dancing together might as well have been in the nude. Even worse, once he finished his dance with her, he forced me to dance with him. Forced me — giving me no choice despite my pleas. It mortified me. My first days in the United States felt unnatural.

In the tumultuous year of 1969 and at the trying age of 13, I found myself in a new country, new culture, new city, new home, new school, new everything. Every step I took felt as if I were walking on shifting ground. Nothing looked or felt familiar, leaving me adrift in a sea of newness. To make matters worse, my father had chosen for us to live in an adult-only apartment complex, Knob Hill, in the Atlanta suburb of Sandy Springs, and it was difficult to try to make any friends that summer. I was told our stay in the apartment was only until Daddy could find a job here in the States, or possibly, Spain.

The smaller of the two swimming pools in the sprawling apartment complex was right outside my bedroom window. I would sit at the window and watch all the young adults play in the pool, drink beer or cocktails, and flirt with each other. It was all so foreign to me and an introduction to U.S. culture and customs.

My parents and I had a difficult time adjusting to the close quarters, however temporary. I spent my life in a house and neighborhood where I could disappear for hours at a time in Argentina; I lived independently with the freedom to travel pretty much anywhere I could catch a bus or train or, even at times, rely on Don Sereno to take me. My parents rarely knew where I was or what I was doing, and they said nothing as long as I showed up at dark. Being in constant contact with my parents seemed foreign and overwhelming — it felt like I was interacting with unfamiliar people.

Usually, Alberta knew where I was first headed, and that was enough. During my younger years, I'd often spend my allowance on toys and trinkets for my Barbie family, which I found at local novelty shops. As I grew older, these jaunts transitioned into opportunities to meet up with friends at the ice cream store. Later still, I found I enjoyed taking my allowance to go shopping, especially when I could take the colectivos down to Domingo Repetto and wander in and out of the myriad of local shops. I especially loved the shoe stores — the smell of leather delighted my senses.

Now, in this small apartment in Atlanta, we had no choice but to be crammed together day and night. My father started out with an optimistic outlook about Atlanta, the up-and-coming city of the South that it was, but soon his mood shifted. He couldn't find a job. He was overqualified for anything that suited his skills and, at 54, too old to start something new. As time went on, he became more and more depressed about his unexpected and prolonged unemployment. There would be glimmers of hope along the way, ones he would share with me and Mother. The position at Data Processing looked promising, and he took pride in keeping us updated on his application status. When Data Processing didn't work out, he found a new possibility. A business executive from South Africa needed my father's expertise in law to help him purchase hotels for investment purposes. My father spent years working for this man, driven by the promise of a financial return. It never came. The company went under before it could make any profits. My dad gave up at that point. He did, however, practice his law skills further in the coming years, as he sued Merrill Lynch for wrongful trading strategies. He won. Unprecedented, especially for the time.

My mother, accustomed to having household help around all the time, now had to revive her long unused cooking and cleaning skills. She worked tirelessly in the tiny kitchen, preparing three meals a day for my father. And after spending my whole life eating meals in the kitchen with the house staff, I was now expected to eat in the dining area with my parents. It was beyond awkward for me. I sat quietly and spoke only when necessary. Often, I'd let my mind drift to happier times. Nothing felt right.

Everything was unfamiliar and unsettling as I entered a whole new world. I could only hope that once school started, and I built a new life there, I would feel somewhat normal again. Despite the dismal circumstances, hope remained my steadfast ally.

My sister Ivette spent her summer off from college with us, sleeping in the third bedroom. Her presence for a couple of months brought a welcome and enjoyable distraction. One day, while Ivette was hanging out with me in my bedroom, my mother came in to drop off some laundry. She spotted something on the carpet. Frantically, she grabbed the Seventeen magazine Ivette and I were checking out, wadded it up, and whacked at the floor with wild fervor. "It's a roach," she yelled. "A huge roach!" Ivette and I laughed hysterically. With tears running down our faces, we couldn't stop cracking up long enough to let her know she had just killed the black top to a Bic pen.

Ivette hung out at the complex pools and met all kinds of people. She even dated a Vietnam vet a few times, who was missing both legs and wore prosthetics. People were drawn to her open mind and chipper demeanor. I admired her. One night, she took me over to a psychic's apartment within the complex, that she had met and chatted with at the big pool.

It was thrilling to meet this woman, whose abode was as mystical as she was. True to the reputation, there was an instant welcoming of incense wafting about, black lights glowing, purple velvet drapes kissing the floor, flickering candles, magic glass balls, and best of all, Miss Vivian herself. She wore a long, flowing black skirt with a white blouson top. Her black locks of hair with red lipstick and nails had her looking the part perfectly. "How are you dear Ivette!" she exclaimed. "This must be your precious younger sister, Stephanie, that you were telling me about," she continued.

"Yes," Ivette responded cheerfully, glad to be making the introductions. Charmed from the start, I found Miss Vivian enchanting, inspiring and gifted in the art of mysticism. She read my Tarot cards briefly.

"Your new school will be a little scary at first, but you will assimilate just fine. Make sure you find your band of people — they will accept you right away..." I left there that night with even more respect for my open-minded, cool sister, not realizing it would be the last time I would get to be with her as she was. By the time I saw her next, she was married and well on her way to transforming into the conservative Christian enthusiast she was destined to be.

Ridgeview High School, which I attended for eighth grade, was brand new, giving me hope I wouldn't be the only new kid. As we all gathered in the auditorium on the first day of class, I met Tess, who was also new to the school. From what I could tell, all the other students had already established connections from previous years together at other schools in the area. Tess was a gorgeous blonde with perfectly round, perky eyes, and I knew she would soon have new friends flocking to her side. I, on the other hand, was as ordinary as it gets. Despite my thin, athletic build, my face lacked any distinctive features and appeared rather plain. Large head and ears, long dark dull hair, small almond eyes, freckles, red cheeks, and a nose I thought was too big.

On the first day during homeroom, I made my first gaffe. When roll was being called, mine was one of the first few names announced, and I responded just as I had my whole life. "Present." The class snickered. I noticed that all the American kids responded with "here," or "yeah," when their names were called. My flushed face started to return to normal when the teacher announced that I was new from Argentina. Indiscernible murmurs and comments floated through the room, and the entire class turned to stare at me, igniting my face all over again. I heard one student say arrogantly, "So you're Argentine, not American."

With a hesitant voice, I explained though I was American, I had lived in Argentina. I wanted to disappear into my chair.

It was hard for me not to notice that I was cheaply dressed compared to my classmates. Most of the girls wore J. Crew, Ralph Lauren, Brooks Brothers, Polo, and Sassoon — brands I did not know but soon learned. Meanwhile, I wore a mix of thrift store finds, Kmart brand, and Lerner's clothes. In my new reality, only Villager or Aigner purses were acceptable, and there was no way I was going to be sporting a $100 purse anytime. I was sensitive enough to recognize what a waste of money that was.

It didn't occur to me that my father's being out of a job contributed to our having to be so cheap. My mother had always been frugal, even when we lived in affluence. She never bought us clothes from department stores but had a seamstress, Angela, come into our home and make our clothes. The weight of judgement bore down on me. So much for an acceptable first day.

Still so homesick for Argentina and my life there, I found an unfamiliar set of standards in the States — completely opposite of what I was used to and who I was. In Argentina, being nicer to others, putting effort toward academics, and being a group participant garnered you more friends and popularity. Here in the States, I quickly learned that shallowness measured one's popularity, and those who triumphed also had the most expensive clothes, homes, and toys. Who you were as a person didn't matter as much as what you could flaunt materialistically. I felt lost here. There was no way I could make such a monumental shift.

Being 1969, the worldwide hippie movement was well under way, and the school had its fair share. They were a quirky bunch, including misfits and the downtrodden, but I always enjoyed people who were unique and authentic. I started hanging out in the hippie area of the school. Pods of people — preppies, jocks, rednecks, and hippies grouped according to social status — littered the front of our school. The hippies were by far the most real and accepting group, and that's where I landed.

My grades reflected my depression. My focus shifted to making friends, and I neglected my studies. What was the point? I no longer needed to make Daddy proud, and my peers didn't seem to care at all about grades. They already nicknamed me a bookworm and a nerd. I needed to dispel the negative labels. Before my grades started plummeting, I had tested out of eighth-grade math and was placed into a special small class taking Algebra I. It was the only class where I managed good grades and that was only because our football coach teacher blasted me in front of everyone one day. "Stephanie, why did you get an 'F' on your test?" he blurted out to the class as he passed out our graded tests. "I *know* you get this material. You are just choosing not to apply yourself!" I blushed feverishly as he tossed the test onto my desk with a big red "F" emblazoned at the top. I may not have cared much about grades anymore, but I did not like being humiliated in front of a class full of people I didn't even know. "You had better step up your game in this class, because I won't tolerate your insolence," he continued.

Please just stop, I thought. *I get it. Just stop already.* His berating, bluntness, and rudeness prompted a sense of fear in me. These were not the intelligent, diplomatic teachers that reigned at ACS in Argentina. These under-appreciated teachers didn't seem to want to be there any more than we did. I was totally stunned to see the way students talked back to teachers. I had experienced nothing like it in Argentina. My world was flipped upside down, and I had a lot of trouble coming to terms with it. I did, however, start making A's in Coach's algebra class.

I begged my parents repeatedly to let me go back to Argentina, but they turned me down every time I brought it up. At last, my mother sat me down one day and explained the situation we were in.

"Stephanie," she started out as I ate my after-school snack. "In Argentina the laws about American business people working in the country only allowed an American to work at a company for two years. Then you had to leave. That is why many of your friends were only there for two years." I thought about what she said and realized she was right. *Melissa Long had only been there for two years. So had Jackie and Janet's family.* "Because PASA Petroquimica wanted to hang on to Daddy and his important work for them, they would change Daddy's official title every two years as a way of keeping him there," she continued. "After seven years, the government caught up with him and they insisted he needed to leave." She paused a moment to let all of that sink in. "So you see, we had to leave." I finally realized how futile all my begging to stay there had been.

"But why couldn't I stay there with another family," I persisted.

"Argentina is going through some difficult political times, Stephanie, and it is not safe to live there right now. We would be negligent parents to allow you to live there under these current circumstances." There it was. My quest to go back to Buenos Aires was finished, no matter how much pleading I engaged in. I felt desperate to make friends here in the States. I was tired of being homesick and lonely and needed to press forward.

Bobby Smith was the first guy who paid any real attention to me, and he quickly became my boyfriend. He hung out with the hippie kids, had longish hair, and was missing part of one of his front teeth. What he lacked in looks, he made up for in personality, and that was what counted for me. Bobby was fun and funny, and I picked up on that pretty quickly outside in the hippie area of school, where we hung out after classes. Bobby approached me one day. "Stephanie, do you want a ride home with me today so you can stay past bus line and hang out for a while?" Longing for a diversion, I accepted. We chatted all the way home to the apartment, and it wasn't long before we became an item.

Bobby loved music and aspired to be a radio DJ one day. He often played sets of music he had expertly put together over the phone for me. Bobby planned his music choices carefully.

Once Bobby was my boyfriend, life felt a little better for me. I finally had someone to love who loved me back. Bobby, 16, was two years older than me. He worked as a dishwasher and busboy at a select steakhouse in Sandy Springs, The Torch and Candle, after school and on weekends. When not in school, I hung out in the restaurant kitchen and took breaks with Bobby. It was there I met Jessica, a server, who needed a babysitter from time to time.

Jessica hired me to babysit her two boys — Steve, seven, and Brandon, a darling baby of just a few months. I fell in love with these boys. It felt so good to have a family of my own. I could play real live house with my two precious boys. Since Bobby knew the family and introduced me, he felt welcome to visit me anytime I babysat the boys. It completed my virtual family — husband and children. All there for me to love and to get love. I finally started to feel better about living in the States.

I babysat almost every weekend and sometimes on weeknights. Bobby was a cigarette smoker, and it wasn't long before I was, too. Despite his protests, I lit up a Marlboro Red, and that's all it took. Another first was sex. Bobby assured me that as soon as I was 16, he could marry me, so having sex would not be bad for us. I went along with it. He was responsible enough to take me to the free clinic behind the Crisis Center to get some birth control pills. It was located around 10th and Peachtree streets, at the heart of "the strip," where the midtown hippies lived and hung out. I was now camped out on the entrance floor, awaiting my new fate, next to where it all began. The paradox was almost comical. I'd gone full circle.

Sex meant little to me at that age. A quasi-Catholic girl—I had my first communion and confirmation—I carried a lot of guilt about allowing Bobby to have sex with me. It was a means of making him happy, and that meant he would stay with me. Just find someone to love me and be loyal.

Trying to fill the enormous hole left in my heart from leaving Argentina, I wasn't as focused on grades, but rather on friendships, and then my school situation improved. I met Marilyn. Her boyfriend, Hal, was one of Bobby's best friends. We went to football games mostly to hang out with each other. The same goes for local friends' parties. They provided us unsupervised spaces to be ourselves, eat junk food, listen to music, and dance. I was so happy to have a close friend again. You could find the four of us at Chastain Park in the amphitheater almost every weekend, living the hippie life as fully as we could. We saw many bands there, including a young up-and-coming group called Three Dog Night.

Our P.E. teacher, Miss Manning, pulled me aside one day and suggested that I try out for cheerleading the following year. "Stephanie, I've been watching you closely, and I am confident that your talents and athletic abilities would qualify you to get onto the cheerleading squad next year. I hope you'll consider it seriously and let me know if I can set you up for tryouts when they come around."

Stunned into silence, I finally answered back, "I'd like to try out. I used to love gymnastics in Argentina and was a part of my school's team. Thanks." I was elated. The news was so uplifting, it filled me with excitement and ambition for the future. Landing a spot on the cheerleading squad would surely expand my social circle and improve my overall emotional state.

15
IT'S OVER

"Stab the body and it heals, but injure the heart and the wound lasts a lifetime." - Mineko Iwasaki

*D*uring the summer of 1970, my life took an unexpected and crushing turn. As I babysat Jessica's boys one Friday night, Steve approached me sheepishly soon after I arrived at their apartment. "I know a secret that I'm not supposed to tell you," he said cheekily.

"You, do, huh?" I answered, grinning and chuckling, covering up the angst that was quickly creeping around my gut.

"Uh, huh," he responded.

"Well, why aren't you supposed to tell me this secret?" I prodded.

"Because it'll make you sad," he answered matter-of-factly.

Adrenaline seeped its way through me. "Well, I think I'll be more sad if you don't tell me what it is. I promise I'll be fine, okay?" I encouraged him.

Steve hemmed a bit and then blurted out, "Bobby went to Six Flags with us and he and Aunt Sammie were kissing. There's even a picture of it."

My world fragmented. I wanted out of my body. *Observe this from the outside and don't crumble*, I told myself. *You have to take care of the boys, you can't fall apart. Just hold it together the best you can, please*, I thought to myself. "Where's the picture? Can you show it to me?" I beseeched him.

Steve scoured through a drawer in the walnut-finished end table and retrieved a large envelope with the familiar Walgreens Photos logo. He shuffled through the pictures and found the one he wanted, cautiously handing it to me. There at Six Flags was my boyfriend Bobby, kissing Jessica's younger sister, Samantha, who was visiting from Michigan. My world was completely torn apart. The level of devastation I felt was beyond what words can describe. It's an all-encompassing dread and fear combined with loathing and despair. I was dispensable and unwanted. Feeling like I needed to curl up in the fetal position on the floor, I couldn't give my anguish the attention it begged from me. Bobby's whispered words of love and promises of forever had convinced me we would be married someday. Here he was kissing a girl he barely knew at the log ride.

"Why did Bobby go to Six Flags with y'all?" I asked, hoping for some insight into this misery I found myself mired in.

"Mom said Bobby could go with us as a date for Aunt Sammie," Steve shared.

I couldn't imagine what I might have done to Jessica. Why would she have secretly set up my boyfriend with her sister? I felt unbelievably betrayed. And how could Bobby do this to me? I broke into shivers, hiding my hands so the boys wouldn't see them trembling, only wanting to get home to call Bobby.

Mort, Jessica's husband and the boys' father, returned from work first, and he took me home. It was good that it worked out that way, as I don't think I could have faced Jessica that night. It would be too painful.

I called Bobby within minutes of arriving home. "Hey," I started, "what's up with the visit to Six Flags with Jessica?" hoping he couldn't detect the trembling in my voice.

"What are you talking about?" he feigned innocently.

"You know what I'm talking about. Don't lie to me any more than you already have," I continued, my mouth going dry on me. "I babysat the boys tonight, and Steve told me all about it."

"Oh," he suddenly interjected, almost jovially and hedging his bets. "That. It was no big deal, really. Jessica's sister came into town for a visit and they wanted me to come along to the park so she could hang out and go on rides with someone close to her age."

"So that's it, huh?" I said with obvious disdain. "Nothing happened with you and Jessica's sister?"

"Nope. Nothing. I don't know why you'd think that. I just went along with the family. It was such a non-deal that I forgot to even tell you about it," he tried to convince me.

My body was now quivering along with my voice. My throat constricted as I got out, "Then why is there a picture of you and Samantha kissing?"

The distinct sound of a phone being slammed down echoed through the receiver. I hung my head as I laid the phone back in its cradle. My fleeting hope for a miraculous explanation to clear Bobby was destroyed. Sitting on my bed, I wrapped my arms around my knees, cradling the shell I lived in. I had reached a breaking point. The energy it took to get through each day had been challenging enough. I knew I had no more reserves to pull from to get through his desolating betrayal and to the other side. Trapped in this nightmare, the only thought consuming me was how to escape this hellish place. I tried sleeping, but couldn't. Ruminating through the night's events, I realized my spirit was eroded, and I was losing all hope. Nothing was going right. I would lose everything I had built with Bobby, and I would be alone and lonely again. I decided I would take a bunch of my allergy pills. Just taking one would make me so sleepy ... maybe if I took a bunch of them, I would just fall asleep and never wake up again in this pain filled world. I took around six to eight of them. With some hesitation, I rang Bobby back, half expecting he wouldn't bother to answer, suspecting it was me calling. But, being a family phone, he must have felt compelled to respond to the ringing. "Hello," he answered cautiously.

"It's me. I decided to take some pills to make sure I go to sleep and never wake back up in this fucking cruel world. Happy now?" I retorted angrily. To avoid another call, I immediately hung up and took the phone off the hook. His blatant cheating caused damage, and I wanted him to realize how much torment I was in. I remembered to put the phone back in its cradle before I spaced out. It was close to midnight.

The next morning, both of my parents tried to wake me, but I didn't want to get up. I couldn't walk on my own. They hung my arms around their necks and walked me around the apartment. They kept asking me what was wrong. I couldn't tell them. They said Bobby had been trying to call me and he finally told them I had taken a bunch of pills. Obviously, my feeble attempt at suicide didn't work. Now it was just going to be worse. My parents would not let up. They kept pressing me about what was wrong, but I was steadfast. All I could tell them was how much I hated my life here in the States. I only wanted to go home to Argentina.

The following week, my mother told me to get dressed to go shopping for school clothes. Daddy would go with us because he needed to pick up his altered clothes at the mall. However bizarre that was, I was glad to be getting new clothes. After years of wearing uniforms, the freedom to wear my own clothes was a big deal. Maybe they were trying to help me feel better about life?

We didn't go to the mall. We drove up to a brick office building. It was then I was told we were actually going to see a psychologist. I was so pissed off. I couldn't believe my mother had lied to me. And I couldn't believe my father had agreed to see a psychologist. He considered them all to be charlatans.

I fumed in the waiting room of the psychologist's office and refused to speak to my parents. Knowing how my father felt, I knew my mother must have convinced him this was the only way. I felt insulted they brought me here under false pretenses. When we were called into the overly ornate, antique stuffed office, I found a man close to my parents' age, dressed in a suit and tie, looking like a school principal. I couldn't relate to that old dude at all. My father insisted that he and my mother stay in the office with us, and the psychologist attempted to dialogue with me. "I don't care who you are. My parents lied to me about coming here. We're supposed to be school clothes shopping at the mall. There's nothing wrong with me. I just want to go back home to Argentina! I hate it here in the States! My parents are just too old and don't understand me or these times," I almost shouted, my voice shakily raised and emphatic. "All of you can go to hell!" I blurted out before thinking it through. What I said surprised me. Just as my father was also getting out of his chair and voicing to the doctor, "You see what we have to put up with?!" I headed toward the door, taken aback that we were leaving. I thought I'd be doing a solo walkout and here my parents were rising as well, apparently ready to leave. They must have felt as pessimistic as I did. We piled back into Daddy's beloved baby blue Cougar and rode home in deafening silence.

16

THE COLONEL UNHINGED

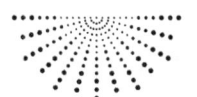

"The most mentally deranged people are certainly those who see in others indications of insanity they do not notice in themselves." - Leo Tolstoy

I was so desperate to hang on to Bobby, even after he cheated on me. *I didn't have anyone else, and now that I was "used," who'd even want me?* It felt dreadful. I felt abysmal. Useless and pathetic. I had to get some answers from Bobby. There were so many questions. My friend Marilyn and I went up to The Torch and Candle restaurant to see Bobby at work. We were back in the kitchen area trying to talk to him while he washed dishes.

Suddenly, we heard a commotion at the back door. My father appeared out of nowhere, swinging a golf club over his head yelling, "He raped my daughter! He raped my daughter!" Bobby bolted from the kitchen through the dining room with night customers enjoying their meals. My father was running after him, the golf club above his head, screaming, "He raped my daughter! He is a child rapist!" The guests, utterly bewildered and shocked by the sudden chaos that had erupted, stopped eating, and murmured amongst themselves, their surprise discernible.

By the time Bobby and my father rounded the dining room corner and headed toward the back door, the chef came out of the kitchen and met them with his gun. Everything stopped and went into extreme slow motion. Chef raised his arm straight ahead, pointed his large silver gun at my father, and demanded, "Get the hell out of here. Now." I watched my father reluctantly head out the back door, saying angrily, "But he raped my daughter ..." As he left, I glimpsed my mother sitting in the car, waiting dutifully.

My adrenaline surged. Marilyn and I witnessed and heard it all going down from behind a kitchen work cart where we were crouched low and hidden. My father never even realized we were at the restaurant. Dumbfounded between extreme embarrassment and deep fear, I questioned my father's behavior. *Had he snapped?* I didn't want my father to get shot or killed. That someone had pointed a loaded gun at him ... that it took a gun to stop him scared me. I didn't dare go home.

Marilyn and I left the restaurant and walked to her older brother's house nearby. Her brother, Mark, kept repeating, "You've got to go home. I can't allow you to stay here and not let our parents know you are okay. Look, I'm sorry you guys are scared, but it'll all be okay. I'll call and let everyone know you two are safe and here with me."

My parents soon showed up at Mark's house, and I reluctantly went out and got in the car. For the first time, I felt physically and emotionally vulnerable to the violent behavior I had witnessed in my father. The car ride was devoid of conversation, but I found out what provoked the outrage.

In their quest to find out what had triggered my failed suicide attempt, my parents searched my room. "Stephanie," my mother said in her serious voice. "We went through your bedroom trying to find answers to why you took too much medication that night last week. We found your hidden cigarettes and some birth control pills," she concluded. Everyone my age was doing it back then, so it was no big deal, but I was no longer my father's pure, darling virgin. It was more than he could stand, and he lost it. I felt even worse once the secret was out. My father's extreme reaction left me feeling like a nobody, nothing, vacant, empty. I was "one of those girls," now. Cheap and worthless. I didn't bother responding to my mother. There was nothing I could say. I was incensed at the violation of my privacy. I guess I deserved that shit. This was going to be the beginning of life becoming more complicated.

Once home, my father called me to their room, catching me before I could head down the hallway to my room. I was nervous, not knowing what might be next. Before I knew it, my father shoved me backwards onto his bed, climbed on top of me, straddled my chest with his legs on either side of me, and pinned down my arms. He brought his hands around my neck and started choking me. "No daughter of mine will behave this way!" he screamed as he shook me up and down. My mother, standing nearby, begged him to stop and get off me.

"Gordon! Stop it! Don't hurt her! Please stop!" she yelled, his ears deaf with rage. My instincts were to fight back, and my arms and legs struggled under his body, failing to shove him off.

"You are such a disgrace to this family," he kept on. I could feel myself fading away when my mother finally pulled him off of me and stopped him. I rose by sheer will and with a burst of adrenaline, ran to my bedroom and locked my door. I couldn't even fathom what had just transpired. It was too much. His hatred followed me — I could feel it trying to hunt me down.

17
AUGUSTA, GA - THE ARMY

"Strength and growth come only through continuous effort and struggle." - Napoleon Hill

I holed up in my bedroom for the next couple of days, only to receive the news that I would soon be sent to live with my brother Henry, his wife Regina, and their baby, Lulu. They were living in an apartment in Augusta, Georgia, where my brother was stationed with the Army.

"You will not see that Bobby Smith ever again," my father announced sternly. "We forbid you to, as does his mother. We expect you to start over with Henry and Regina." Boarding a Greyhound bus, I embarked on a journey that led me to a stint of existence in stagnation and oppression. The transition from the bustling metropolis of Atlanta to this unfamiliar town felt like stepping back in time, as if I had entered a world untouched by progress. Henry got me registered and enrolled in the local public school, and I was one of only a handful of white students attending. I didn't care. My life felt so out of control that nothing much mattered.

Living with Henry and Regina wasn't too bad. Although Henry and I had never been tight, we got along fine, and Regina and I only met once. Regina was a petite blonde with a shoulder-length bob that framed her chiseled facial features perfectly. Well coifed, Gina, as she was affectionately called, came from a well-to-do family from the northeast. The kind of money that meant she would never have to work in her lifetime if she chose not to, and indeed, that is what she ultimately settled on. Despite her knowledge of manners, she frequently neglected to use them. Not warmhearted by nature, she was icy and aloof. Most of the family tolerated her but didn't befriend her. I was ambivalent, too young to care. She was nice enough to me what few days I had with her during that timeframe.

I had only seen their daughter, Lulu, in photographs, and she became my little angel. She was still a baby, and I relished taking her out for walks in her stroller. I always loved babies and the outdoors, and this provided me with a brief escape into my own small world. I also managed to smoke a cigarette or two on my walks with Lulu. It wasn't long before they figured out I was smoking, and this infuriated my brother. 'Who the hell do you think you are? You can't smoke cigarettes while taking our Lulu out! Have you lost your mind? Obviously that's the only reason you even take her out for a walk." My moments with my precious little niece helped fill the empty space from no longer having little Steve and baby Brandon to take care of. *Did they wonder where I was?* I didn't have the will left in me to mount a defense against my brother's accusations. When Henry said I was taking the first Greyhound bus back, I just gave in. I lasted two weeks in Augusta.

At least I would leave Augusta with some fashion credibility in my next small town home. Gina had taken me clothes shopping shortly after I arrived in Augusta. I found the most incredible taupe suede, knee-high boots with long suede fringe around the calves. The fringe swung with each sassy step. Regina loved them as much as I did, and it was nice shopping with someone who recognized the day's styles. These boots were the find of the year, and now they were mine.

18
SELMA, AL - THE AIR FORCE

"Love means to love that which is unlovable; or it is no virtue at all." - G. K. Chesterton

Further fed up with me, my father then decided I would live with my oldest brother, Gordy, and his newly expectant wife, Marie. I always looked up to and admired my oldest brother, and I loved his beautiful wife Marie, whom I had known since childhood days in Argentina. As a pilot in the Air Force, Gordy was now firmly rooted in his career. He was our family's Golden Child, and surely this latest attempt at dealing with me, the proverbial black sheep, would work. Gordy was stationed in Selma, Alabama — a tiny town south of Montgomery where John Lewis famously led a march across the Edmund Pettus Bridge, protesting for voting rights in America. On that day, law enforcement beat many civil rights marchers, and it became known as Bloody Sunday.

At least at an Air Force base, kids hailed from all over the States, not just Alabama. The local public school, with its worn-out brick walls and faded paint, left a lot to be desired. The sight of cracked windows and overgrown weeds outside the entrance inspired little confidence. But with no other option available, I braced myself for the experience. The sounds of squeaky lockers and echoing footsteps filled the dark, humid hallways. Despite the less than ideal conditions, I was determined to make the best of it, hoping to find some hidden gems within the vast mediocrity.

In Selma I was a big city girl from Atlanta. My suburban clothes from Lerner's, new, cool suede boots and city girl savvy made me popular. I made friends easily. It was hard to fathom that life was starting to feel enjoyable once more, and maybe I could at last find my sense of belonging.

After arriving in Selma, I received a letter from Bobby Smith, whom I hadn't seen in almost six weeks. My brother brought it to me, "Stephanie, I'm sorry this letter is open, but Daddy insisted I read it to him before giving it to you." I took the letter into my room to read it and wept. Bobby said he had been counseling with his pastor, and he said, among other things, "... you must break all ties with this girl — she is a bad influence on you." I was so hurt by the implication. Like I was the unacceptable one. *How the fuck dare he?* It spurred me to move on from Bobby, but not without severe, lasting damage to my self-esteem. It became more difficult to stave off the self-loathing that drifted right behind me incessantly, following me like a shadow I couldn't ditch.

The only school in our area housed a wide range of students, from country hicks to military officer's children and everything in between. I was frustrated at finding out girls still could not wear pants to school in this backward part of the country. I organized a protest where all of us girls would wear pants to school, and we would sit in the hallway outside the principal's office. When he came out to find us all there, I spoke to him on behalf of our group. We were asking for approval to wear pants to school, as the skirts and dresses policy was severely antiquated. The principal said he understood our point and would take it up with the school board, who had the ultimate authority over our request. In the meantime, we had to change our clothes and put dresses or skirts on according to the current dress code, he instructed.

We had covered that base already. We went back to our respective classes and dropped our pants, leaving nothing but our long T-shirts on that were within their guidelines of three inches above the knee. Our protest was well received.

Within a few weeks, the board approved our request, and we achieved our goal, a victory that gave me some urban credibility.

My Selma friends and I spent weekends partying in dilapidated abandoned houses in wide, empty fields that surrounded the bleak and blighted area. We smoked pot and drank beer if we could score it. Music roared through portable radios, while boys burned farts, typical teen bullshit for the times.

I started going steady with a great-looking guy, Matthew. He went to another school, so we saw each other on weekends. As the lead singer in a local rock band, I loved how he would sing to me from the stage during shows. He expressed his desire to marry me and insisted we couldn't ruin that with premarital sex. I cared little about sex. I found it boring and messy, so it was a relief that this would not be a thing with Matthew.

When Christmas season arrived, my mother came down to Selma to "babysit" me while Gordy and Marie went to her family's home for the holidays. We managed fine until it was time for her to head home. There would be a weekend overlap, and I was to go back to Atlanta with her. My brother would then pick me up in Atlanta and bring me back to Selma with him. I didn't want to go. I was still upset with Daddy and didn't want to see him, and I wanted to hang out with my friends while we were off from school, not spend it in a car all weekend. On the day we were to leave, I hid at a friend's house to avoid my mom. I called her and told her I would not be going back to Atlanta with her; I was staying at a friend's. "You can't just stay away, Stephanie. You must come back and ride to Atlanta with me. I can't just leave you here without any adult supervision," my mother pleaded.

"I have no plans to come back to the house. You might as well leave without me, 'cuz I'm not coming back," I calmly told her. I knew I had the upper hand. She would never find me and needed to leave soon. After a few rounds back and forth, she finally gave up and left without me. I returned to the empty house, relieved. She was gone. Everyone was gone, and I could enjoy some longed-for time alone.

I invited a group of close friends to hang out at my brother's house that Saturday night with no adults at home. When Saturday came around, not only did my close friends arrive, but plenty of older teens I didn't even know. They kept filing in, armed with booze and pot. When munchies set in, they opened a veritable restaurant in the kitchen, finding things to cook. By the time the party was over, I faced an enormous mess to clean up on my own in the wee hours of the morning. I didn't know what time Gordy and Marie were due back that Sunday. Hours of effort paid off as the house finally regained its original appearance.

I failed to get it as clean as I thought I had. Gordy discovered a used condom in their bedroom and realized I had a party in their absence. Although I felt deep shame, my pride and fear prevented me from the humbling experience I needed.

In the spring of 1971, Gordy and Marie were expecting their first child and needed their space. They had tolerated me long enough and deserved to have their lives back. I was sure the party didn't help my cause, but they never let on that it had sullied our relationship. They told me that Daddy reimbursed them for all the food and steaks that came up missing. I was sure he'd be furious about having to pay for the lost food.

The prospect of moving back in with my parents filled me with dread. I finally found a place that felt like home and had made good friends. Another upheaval meant leaving everything I worked hard to build in the past six months, including my boyfriend, Matthew. The urge to give up overcame me again. I was tired of being shuffled around like an inconvenient interloper.

I don't even remember going back to school in Atlanta. Deeply depressed and filled with despair, I no longer cared about anything, least of all myself. I knew I was an annoyance to my parents, and they were trying to dump me on someone, anyone. I was so confused. None of my behavior deviated from that of my peers — smoking pot, going to parties, and every girl I knew was having sex while I wasn't even in a sexual relationship and hadn't been since Bobby. Somehow, their parents didn't want to get rid of them, but mine were adamant. I was not fulfilling my parents' aspirations for me. Depressed and angry, I became defiant, and that was grounds for exile. I turned 15 in late March 1971, but none of us felt like celebrating much of anything. Back in the States for almost two years, Daddy still didn't have a job, and Mother continued to make sure we lived frugally.

19
PACK YOUR FAVORITE THINGS

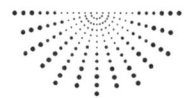

"The loneliest moment in someone's life is when they are watching their whole world fall apart, and all they can do is stare blankly." - F. Scott Fitzgerald

The afternoon was waning at the Crisis Center. The atmosphere was thick with visible emotions. Tired faces, slumped shoulders, sighs, hushed conversations, sweat, patchouli, cigarette smoke, and exhaustion—all contributed to the palpable weariness hanging heavy in the air after a long day. My body ached from sitting on the concrete for so long. Connie came by to check on me a couple of times. She said we'd leave soon to go to her apartment, and I thought back to how the day had started off.

That morning, my father came into my room and ordered

me to get up. "Stephanie, get out of bed right now. You need to pack a bag with anything of yours that you want to keep. Don't argue with me or say anything. Be ready to leave here in thirty minutes."

Disoriented and perplexed, I rubbed my face as I tried to catch up to my father's abrupt words. *Where were we going? Were we taking a trip I didn't know about?* I glanced down the narrow hallway and saw no other suitcases. *Was I being shipped off to that boarding school in Virginia they tried to sell me on?* My mind was reeling, flooded by a deluge of thoughts and emotions. The world seemed to blur before my eyes. A knot was forming in my stomach, a physical manifestation of the turmoil I felt inside. I got the small blue suitcase out of my closet and started adding clothes to it. Packing my jewelry box, which held all my treasures, took up a chunk of space, so I was limited in how many clothes I could bring. Wearing my favorite worn-out side-studded flare jeans and a yellow knit top with purple flower trim, I was ready. I got my purse, the suitcase, and grabbed my guitar on the way out of my room. Mother was standing at the front door, her eyes welling up with tears. She hugged me and said goodbye. I almost started tearing up but was so caught up in fear that I stifled all other feelings. Despite all our recent disagreements, I hated to see her sad, much less on the verge of crying. I couldn't imagine what was going on. Wherever we were going, she wasn't coming with us.

My father drove in silence, and I stared out the car as we drove south on Roswell Road, toward the city. It was a bright, cloudless spring day in Atlanta, a morning when I would have likely caught a ride to Chastain Park to hang out with friends. Instead, here I was heading to unknown destinations with my father, who I was convinced had gone full-blown mad by this point. He was not the same man I had known growing up.

Completely intolerant of everyone and everything, he was open to rages and depressed. He was no longer the composed, intelligent, quirky man I revered as a small child. I was incredibly sad to no longer admire and respect my father. I missed that. A lot. I wondered if he ever missed his little Nena, too.

As we arrived, I spotted the Atlanta Crisis Center — its location on Peachtree Street between 10th and 14th was instantly recognizable. Ironically, it was in front of the building that housed the free clinic where Bobby got my birth control pills. My father parked the car, and we walked into the center, leaving my stuff in the trunk.

Were we here for counseling? Why did I have to bring a packed suitcase? A center counselor, who introduced herself as Connie Fulbert, greeted us. She led us to her tiny, cluttered office and asked how she could help as she gestured for us to sit across her shabby wooden desk.

My father handed Connie one of his business cards and started, "My daughter here is a rebellious, incorrigible teenager. She won't listen to us or follow our rules. We don't want her living with us anymore."

"Colonel Flynn," Connie attempted to interject, "We often find teenagers to be a challenge at this stage...."

"No," the Colonel interrupted. "You didn't hear me clearly. She's not welcome to stay in our home any longer. Stephanie has been nothing but a problem to her mother and me. She doesn't try in school anymore. She smokes cigarettes and meets boys at parks against our rules. We even found birth control pills hidden in her room!"

Connie, ever so professionally, responded, "Colonel Flynn, I'm glad you brought Stephanie here, we can work with both of you to start a communication process ..."

"This kind of behavior is not tolerable in my house," my father continued, talking over her.

Connie tried to explain that although the center was there for counseling, it had no facilities to house anyone. "I'll be right back," he said, dismissing her with agitation. My father got up from his chair, went out the side door to the car, and returned with my suitcase and guitar. Back in Connie's office, he put them both down by the door, turned around, and left without another word.

I had been sitting quietly while my father and Connie discussed me. Connie seemed to be in her early 20s, an attractive woman, cool, diplomatic, street and book smart. She was tall, with long brown hair that waved past her shoulders and down her back. Her large doe eyes were dark brown and striking. Dressed in jeans and a dashiki top with leather sandals, she came across as genuine. I liked and respected her instinctively. In that moment, as I watched Connie's utter disbelief unfold before my eyes, an overwhelming wave of empathy washed over me; I felt deeply sorry for what she was experiencing. She hadn't asked for this. My unhinged father dumped me here with her, and now I was her burden. Guilt and embarrassment slowly made their way through me, the shame I felt settling onto my shoulders.

Connie found her supervisor, Vincent. I couldn't hear their conversation, but when she came back to her desk, Connie said I'd go home with her after work. She showed me where I could wait for her, in the front entrance of the center — a waiting area marked by its dull, hand-printed walls, worn-out unmatched chairs that were partially filled, and the dozen or so freaks drifting in and out.

Sitting down on the floor and leaning my back against the pitted wall, I felt so empty and lost. Despite the urge to cry, I kept fighting back tears. I sat there staring out the front window, wondering *what the hell had just happened?* I could almost believe my crazy father leaving me, but I couldn't understand my mother letting me go.

She had tears in her eyes when I last saw her. *Did she try to change my father's mind on this one? Did she willingly go along with this plan?* I racked my brain trying to figure out what triggered this eviction. There hadn't been any fights or arguments lately. As far as I could tell, we were existing the best we could under stressful and depressing circumstances. *What had prompted my father to leave me?* I truly felt unloved and unwanted. To the core. The pain was indescribable — a profound, gut-wrenching despair that transcended any words and left me feeling so vulnerable. My body vacillated between a state of high alert and crippling defeat.

Two or three hours into my wait at the center, a man, in his 30s or 40s, came in and milled around a bit before walking over to approach me. "You look like you could use a meal. Do you want to eat lunch with me across the street at the Rexall counter — my treat?" I don't know what prompted him to ask me. *Who was this man? Had he been watching me? Could he sense my despondency? Had someone told him I had just been thrown out and left here by my father?* Connie was at the front desk, so I got up and asked her, "Can I go get something to eat with that man?" pointing him out. "He said he'd buy my lunch across the street at the Rexall counter."

"Sure. That's fine, but come right back when you're done," she answered. Following the man across Peachtree Street, we entered and sat down across from each other in a red diner booth. If there was a conversation with him, I don't recall it. I had left the house without breakfast, and it was well into the afternoon at this point. I didn't have much of an appetite, but I was grateful to be sitting down, eating a meal with someone. It meant more to me than that kind stranger will ever know. A meal. A sense that someone cared a little. I sat silently eating a tuna sandwich chased with a Coke. I heard the server ask a couple sitting a few tables away what they would like for dessert. When the woman asked what they had available, she rattled off types of pie: "Key lime, strawberry, peach, cherry, apple, blueberry, blackberry, banana cream," and on it went.

"She's gonna ask for cherry," I murmured. Sure enough, the woman ordered cherry pie. I wondered for a brief moment how I knew what she'd want, and then polished off my own apple pie. When we finished eating, I meekly thanked the man for the meal and returned to the center. I took up my position on the floor and wall again and resumed staring out the front window, numb and misplaced.

After work, we walked back to Connie's apartment while she talked to me about her roommate, Elsie. Connie and Elsie lived in a one-bedroom, fourth-floor apartment only a few short blocks from the Crisis Center. When we walked in, Connie explained my absurd situation to Elsie. "This is Stephanie. She's 15. Her father left her at the center today," she lamented. "I've brought her home to stay with us for a while until we can figure out what course of action to take next." I caught Elsie rolling her eyes during Connie's explanation of my sudden appearance in their world. "This Colonel Flynn walked into my office with Stephanie and just started having a fit about what an awful teenager she was. 'Incorrigible' was the word he kept using. Personally, I think he is the one with a problem, not Stephanie, here." A minor victory. There was finally a person who recognized and seemed to understand my plight, showing compassion for the difficulties I'd been facing.

"What are you thinking is the next step for her?" Elsie asked.

"Well, it damn sure can't be the juvie system — it's broken," Connie answered her.

"I'm guessing no cops were involved," Elsie wondered aloud.

"Oh hell no," Connie replied quietly. "Vince and I decided it was best for her to come back here with me. We'll work on figuring out the rest, soon. Until then, she'll stay here with us."

Elsie brought her attention back to me and voiced her concerns aloud. "Stephanie, you'll have to earn your keep here. You're not going to be freeloading off us. I expect you to help with cleaning and cooking, understood?"

"Yes," I responded nervously. From our first meeting, Elsie's assertive personality intimidated me, and I minded myself when in her presence.

Out of fear for my well-being, Connie staunchly refused to surrender me to the authorities, dreading the possibility of my being thrust into the foster care network or, worse yet, the flawed juvenile system of that era.

I talked openly and honestly with Connie and Elsie. Connie felt safe. I let her know I smoked pot on weekends, had taken speed a few times in Alabama, and took birth control pills in the past while I was with Bobby. I described the last couple of years, leaving nothing out. She assured me I was a normal teen, and that my dad was the crazy one. As good as it felt to receive validation, to be understood that I wasn't an awful person, it didn't change my dire circumstances. I was now homeless and parentless, unwanted by my family. I was certain my parents sought my siblings' approval before abandoning me. Under the blanket, I cried myself to sleep on Connie's couch that night, and the emotional release was welcome. Well-practiced in the art of silent weeping, I choked back sobs so as not to alert Connie or Elsie of my despair. I would put on a false bravado for their sakes.

Being a weekend, Connie was off the next day, and Elsie made it clear to me, again, that she expected me to help cook and clean. I was more than happy to help, eager to be of service. I couldn't help but feel like I was intruding on these two women's time and space, and I would do anything they asked of me.

20
THE PARTY

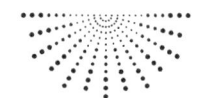

"I just want to sleep. A coma would be nice. Or amnesia. Anything, just to get rid of this, these thoughts, whispers in my mind…" - Laurie H. Anderson

The next night, Connie and Elsie had friends over, a party that had been in the works before my unexpected arrival. About a dozen or more people turned up, and a guy in his 30s came to sit next to me on the couch. David introduced himself, a man with a large muscular build, dark hair, and a full beard. David seemed fully invested in conversing with me, and I riffed on his anecdotes with my own stories. He mentioned an upcoming trip to Brazil, and since I had visited the luscious country, we talked at length about it.

Memories flooded back as I recounted riding in the back

seat of a cab, sandwiched between my siblings, the windows down, allowing the salty beach winds of Ipanema Beach to engulf me. The unmistakable scent of sand filled the air, and the nearby saltwater radiated a soothing warmth. As we zipped through Rio de Janeiro, the dazzling neon lights painted streaks of color across the night.

The party crowd multiplied while Cat Stevens and Joni Mitchell blared from the stereo, eventually rendering conversation impossible. David invited me to his apartment so we could continue our lively discussion in quiet, and he could learn more about Brazil. Surprised to be in demand by a much older guy, I told Connie about David's invite. He was a friend of Elsie's, so Connie checked in with her first and came back to me with a go-ahead.

David and I walked to his apartment, several blocks and turns from Connie's place. He asked me to translate phrases into Spanish for him. I felt so mature and cultured. Living overseas my whole life was proving beneficial. His seemingly genuine interest in me boosted my self-confidence and made me feel valued. I thought we might grow a genuine friendship, despite the considerable age gap, and his attention provided a nice breather from my looming fate.

We entered the older building and walked up a flight of stairs to his apartment door. Once inside, he locked the door. The efficiency apartment had only a single room with a bed, kitchen area, a table and chair, and a bathroom off to one side.

David motioned for me to sit on the bed, while he sat down in the only chair next to the small, worn out Formica dining table to take his socks and shoes off. He continued talking as he stood up and nonchalantly undressed. The hair on the nape of my neck stood up, and I instinctively knew that something was terribly wrong. Before I could even ask him what he was doing, he pushed me backwards onto the metal-framed bed and proceeded to pull off my clothes. His demeanor changed — his actions deliberate and methodical. This was not the guy who had happily chatted with me, sharing stories. He was on a mission, laser-focused. In a cracking, trembling voice, I protested. "I don't want to do this. Please stop. This isn't okay. I'm not on any birth control."

"Shut up," he warned in a deep, fixated voice. He placed his large, heavy legs on mine and pinned my arms down with horrifying efficiency. Adrenaline pulsed through my body, and I fought through the terror, trying to free myself. My struggle led nowhere. I evaluated the situation, and in seconds knew there was no way to overpower this guy. My 5'6", 110-pound frame couldn't compete with his muscular strength. Feeling utterly powerless, I determined my safest bet was to give in. I lay there shaking uncontrollably from the adrenaline and fear coursing through me. Tears streaming down my face, I begged the asshole, "Please stop! I'm not taking any birth control. I don't want to do this. Stop!" He buried his head between my legs. All I could sense was his roughness and the scrape of his thick, scratchy beard against my thighs. Then he positioned himself on top of me and forcefully entered with aggressive thrusts. I shut my eyes and mentally transported myself to a different place, desperate to be anywhere but here, in this moment. When he was done, he rolled over to go to sleep. "Please take me back to Connie and Elsie's apartment now. I really need to get back there. They're going to wonder what happened to me if I don't show back up," I begged him. Looking around for a phone, I didn't see one there. I didn't bother asking if he had one, either. I didn't even know Connie and Elsie's phone number. It had only been one day, and I hadn't gotten far enough for a phone number yet. Damn.

With no remorse and in a ruthless tone, he spat, "Shut up and go to sleep. I'll take you back in the morning." Too afraid to sleep, I wasn't sure if I could find the way back to Connie's. It was late, and I was afraid to wander out on the dark streets alone. I lay there, feeling sick, helpless, and lost. Once again, I found myself crying quietly, trying to understand what had just happened. And why? Why did this older guy want to have sex with me? David had seemed like a decent guy, so why was he now so evil? I felt sure that Connie and Elsie would never have let me go to his house if they didn't think I would be safe with him. I thought about Daddy. What would he think? Is this what he wanted for me? My world continued its descent into the depths of despair, crumbling further into the abyss.

In the morning, David woke up and had me follow him downstairs and outside. He gave me verbal directions to Connie's apartment and sent me on my way. I couldn't wait to get away from him. I felt utter, complete hatred toward this fucker.

As I neared the corner of 10th and Peachtree Street, I had a looming feeling that a car wreck was imminent. Almost in slow motion, two cars approached the intersection at right angles from each other, coming into view as one metallic mass accompanied by deafening screeches and crunching sounds that I barely heard. I stopped to absorb what had happened. The crashing cars mirrored my wrecked life. I started again toward Connie's place, willing my feet one in front of the other.

Connie and Elsie were in the apartment, anxiously awaiting my return. "Where've you been?" Connie blurted out. "We've been so worried about you!"

I slumped into one of the wooden dining chairs, and my shoulders dropped. In a dry, cracking voice, I told the sordid story. "David is a real asshole. He practically ripped my clothes off me and had sex with me. I begged him not to. I kept telling him that I wasn't on any birth control, but he just told me to shut up. I hate him. I didn't have your phone number, and he wouldn't bring me back here last night, either. When he woke up this morning, he took me outside and pointed the way back here."

We sat quietly for a moment, immersed in the shock and absorbing what had transpired the night before. Elsie eventually broke the silence. "I know David a little. He's a Jewish lawyer in town, about 28 years old, I think. What an ass! Next time I see him, I'm going to give him hell, dammit! This is totally fucked up. I sure hope he didn't get you pregnant."

Connie added, "I had no idea he was such a bastard! We're going to get you on some birth control, soon, to keep you safer."

"Would it be alright for me to crash a while on the couch?" I asked. My body was so sore, and my soul so shaken, "I didn't get any sleep last night." Both nodded their heads in understanding.

"Here's a blanket, Steph," Connie offered. I slept for a few hours before waking up enough to recognize I desperately wanted a shower.

21
LIFE AROUND 10TH AND PEACHTREE STREET - THE STRIP

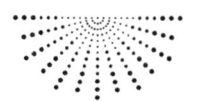

"All great changes are preceded by chaos." - Deepak Chopra

In the following weeks, I spent most days at the Crisis Center, hanging out in the front waiting area while Connie worked in her crammed office in the back. Later in that first week, I ran into a local band member that I knew, Greg. I told him about my situation, and he said he could give me a ride out to Chastain Park to see if any of our friends were there. Connie gave me permission, so off we went. The first and only people I ran into that I knew were a couple of good friends who were a gay couple, Mike and Terry. I told them everything that had transpired over the past week or so. When I told them about the encounter with David, Mike got furious, yelling, "That guy RAPED you! That's rape, dammit! Where does he live? I'm gonna kick his ass!" David was a lawyer, and I feared he would seek retribution, but Mike's concern felt reassuring. I was so alone, and Mike's care and sympathy meant the world to me. He also named it. The vileness had a label.

I lived day by day. Nothing was certain. It was summer, so school was out. Besides, Connie had no legal authority over me and no identification with which to enroll me. My days only took shape when Greg came by to drive me places. I always welcomed his visits because I didn't know anyone in the midtown area and longed for friendly faces.

Sometimes I would hang out with Greg during his band practices, or he would take me to Chastain or Piedmont Park to hang out. When he decided one day that he wanted to have sex with me, I didn't protest. Why bother? I had been reduced to experiencing the trauma of rape. I thought little else could bring me lower. Plus, I felt I owed him for all the visits and running around he did for me. I had no other means of repaying him. Sex would have to do — it was the only currency I had. I learned ongoing lessons about the value of sex to men and the lengths they would go to get it. He did at least use a condom since I was not on any birth control.

My streak of forewarnings continued one day at Chastain Park. Before he turned the key, I knew that Greg's van wouldn't run. "It's not gonna start," I muttered. He freaked out, but it didn't surprise me, as these random premonitions occurred more frequently. Years went by before I understood the link between my intuition and past trauma.

My association with Greg was a fleeting connection that lasted for a few weeks. I finally started meeting some people while hanging out at the Crisis Center and the apartments — people I didn't feel obligated to have thank-you-sex with.

Along with cooking and cleaning at Connie's apartment, I

also learned how to cap mescaline. Connie and Elsie supplemented their meager incomes selling the recreational drug. The three of us sat around the dining table with bowls of the cacti hallucinogen and Nesquik chocolate drink powder. They cut the mescaline with the Nesquik and filled the mixture into empty cellulose capsules. Despite the tedium, I was more than willing to do my part, feeling a sense of purpose with every completed capsule.

When I wasn't at the Crisis Center, I hung out at the apartment and listened to rock radio. I also read anything I could find of interest, including articles and books about the Charles Manson family, big in the day's news. In the evenings, we ate dinner together, talked, read, or listened to music. Connie's friend Lionel Mueller stopped by one evening that summer to catch up with her. He was also their pot dealer. There was an energetic connection between us. Lionel was in his late teens or early 20s, a lanky fellow of average height with long, dirty blond locks and almond-shaped brown eyes. He was an Atlanta transplant from New Jersey and carried himself like a true Jersey native — feisty, self-assured, and sporting a noticeable accent and a chipped incisor. His street-life confidence and positive attitude intrigued me.

Before long, I bummed around midtown with Lionel, as he dealt pot to the locals in the evenings. With Connie's okay, I moved into an apartment with him, just a couple of blocks away from her.

I was excited to be putting together my first place, shopping for household items at K-Mart with Lionel. I was finally creating a home. Lionel and I were in love. At 15 years old, I was willing to buy whatever was being sold to me under the guise of caring. Setting up a home in our little apartment while my reefer-dealing boyfriend went to work felt as normal as things could get for me.

I desperately needed to feel loved by someone, and Lionel adored me, and I reciprocated in return. I was grateful for that perceived love. Our one-room apartment with a bathroom and kitchen sat a block behind 10th and Peachtree Street. Outside our main room window, a plaque read, "Margaret Mitchell lived here when she wrote Gone with the Wind." I couldn't believe the synchronicity. I had heard stories since childhood about the friendship between the Flynn family and Margaret Mitchell. My great Aunt Agnes worked with her at the Atlanta Journal-Constitution. Aunt Agnes invited Margaret for weekends at the family home in nearby Rome. My great Aunt Janie, renowned for her unparalleled kindness, inspired the character of Melanie in the epic southern tale. I was living in the house where Mitchell wrote Gone With the Wind. It felt surreal.

Grand parties in the house were evocative of Mitchell's book. The two gay men who occupied the apartment downstairs knew how to throw a stately affair. The impeccable cross-dressers caught everyone's attention, and their elaborate headdresses were a visual delight. Lionel and I shared an entrance with the couple and were witnesses to the fancy costumes and exquisitely made-up faces. We never complained about the noise going well into the wee hours of the following mornings, and they never said a word about the incessant playing of Neil Young's "Helpless," on the stereo upstairs.

Weeks before meeting Lionel, Connie sent me to the free clinic to get birth control. Their new policy required a pregnancy test before prescribing birth control. I approached the desk at the clinic, where a woman asked how she could help me.

"I need to get a pregnancy test, please, so I can get birth

control pills," I responded meekly. She reached under her desk to retrieve a plastic cup with a screw top and handed it to me.

"Take this cup to the bathroom over there," she pointed. "Pee in it and screw the lid on. Bring it back here to me and I'll put your name on it. Before you do that, sign in, right here." She handed me a clipboard. I did as she said, feeling so embarrassed and nervous. I dreaded the entire process. It was humiliating. As I aimed my pee into the cup, it overflowed, and I was saturated in my own yellow sea of urine. I grabbed the rough toilet paper and desperately tried to wipe away the evidence.

A brown paper bag appeared in the next stall like a lifeboat. Catlike, I pulled the bag over with my foot and placed my pee cup in it. I trotted confidently to the desk and placed my brown paper bag in front of the lady. To my horror, the cap came off, and the cup spilled through the bag onto her desk, drenching it with my piss — wrecking all the papers on her desk. Bystanders in the waiting area turned their attention to the scene that had just unraveled. My mind went blank as a wave of panic washed over me. Disassociating, sweat soaked my face and scalp, while the woman maintained her cool. I went into full meltdown mode, and though she tried to assure me that all was okay, I felt myself drifting out like a boat slowly floating away. "It's okay," the clerk assured as my world crumbled around me. "We've got enough of a sample left to run the test." I can't even remember how I skulked out of the place.

Within a week, Connie came home from work one evening to find me and Elsie talking in their bedroom. "I have some concerning news, Stephanie," she started out. "Your pregnancy test came back today, and it is positive." Her words muddled into nonsense, and I realized spilling my pee should have been an omen.

The energy in the room was thick, knowing that the present

situation was a direct and unavoidable outcome of the rape, a recognition that hung heavy and oppressive like a persistent fog. The timing was accurate, and the shock that I was steadily becoming more and more acquainted with turned me numb.

"We're going to need to get you an abortion, Stephanie," Connie said quietly.

"Yeah," Elsie added. "Given your age and situation, becoming a mother at this point in your life would be disastrous."

"I get it," I responded. I knew I couldn't possibly be responsible for a baby right now. As much as I loved babies, there was no way I was ready to be a mother. I couldn't even take care of myself yet.

"When I see him next," Elsie seethed, "I'm going to give David fucking hell for this. Getting a teenager pregnant, the bastard!" Filled with frustration, she added, "That asshole is going to have to pay for this abortion as well!"

I faced the undeniable need to have an abortion, a decision that was understood implicitly, but it was 1971, and abortions were illegal in Georgia, which complicated the situation enormously.

Elsie knew a nurse in Boston who performed abortions. She got on the phone and found out that Leona would be in Atlanta in the coming months, and they arranged the procedure for me when she came to the city. It was possible that it might be too late, but it was the only option available to us. It was too much to absorb and assimilate, and I couldn't help but retreat into denial and push any thoughts about it out of my mind. I would worry about it when the time came. Accepting my fate, I buried my feelings.

I was growing up rapidly and needed to gain some street skills quickly. My survival instincts were surfacing, with my mind turning on the necessary regions of the brain, when we found ourselves at the bottom of the pyramid. My emotional maturity, on the other hand, ran amok, vacillating between extremes and leaving me feeling vacant and lost.

Sitting on my bed listening to Neil Young's "Helpless" over and over, the song penetrated me deeply, and the knock at the door startled me. A friend of Lionel's stopped by to score some weed, Martin. I could sense his discomfort sitting there with me, waiting for Lionel to return. He sat with his legs crossed and rocked back and forth slowly, chain-smoking his unfiltered Camels, lighting one off of the other and avoiding eye contact. After about five minutes of awkward silence, we finally struck up a conversation, and it was soon obvious to both of us we shared an incredible connection. "I saw Crosby, Stills, Nash & Young at Woodstock," Martin offered, as Neil Young played in the background.

"Wow," I responded, impressed that I'd met someone who had, in fact, been to Woodstock.

"It was actually their second time playing together as a band in public," he continued. "Can you imagine? What a gig for your second time playing together! They were solid — like they'd been playing as a cohesive unit for years."

Martin exuded intelligence and an impressive depth of knowledge on a variety of subjects, including music, the arts, geology, and current events. I was blown away. During our brief visit that day, the unspoken energy between us was palpable. It felt cerebral. In a short while, Lionel returned and took care of Martin's pot order. I could sense his jealousy of Martin's being there alone with me. I knew I would see Martin again, I just didn't know when or where.

One night, after a good day of sales, Lionel wanted to take me somewhere upscale for dinner. We went to a hippie shop on the strip and bought a second-hand dress for me to wear that night. It may not have qualified as dressed up to others, but I felt good in my new yellow satin dress with a sash around the hips and the blouson sleeves. Lionel even got out of his daily seedy, worn clothes and into a nice pair of jeans with a short-sleeved blue and white pin-striped shirt he picked up at the Goodwill store.

We dined at Mario's, a high-end Italian restaurant, and I thoroughly enjoyed a night out somewhere so elegant. The white linen napkins and tablecloths reminded me of formal dinners at home in Buenos Aires. They served table water through a seltzer dispenser — each table had its own.

Before our dinner arrived, in the middle of a conversation, I leaned over to Lionel and whispered, "That seltzer bottle is going to explode," pointing to the table diagonal to ours. Damned if the glass didn't shatter and fly across the diners at the table less than a minute of my uttering those words. Luckily, no one was injured beyond nicks and scratches, but the spray showered them pretty thoroughly. Lionel was taken aback by the sudden minor explosion at the nearby table and was just as surprised that I had predicted it. I shared my recent premonitions with him.

"What I didn't see coming was that my parents would be moving," I said as we waited for our food. "My dad called Connie at work and told her he and my mom moved to Washington, D.C.! Connie was pissed. It doesn't really surprise me, though. My dad doesn't give a shit. He does whatever he wants. Nothing gets or stays in his way."

I found out my parents moved to Washington D.C. a few weeks after leaving me. It didn't surprise Connie as much as appall her that my parents would move out of state mere weeks after dumping me on her. She felt a strong conviction to keep me from the authorities and brainstormed ways to legally separate me from my parents. The simplest plan was to marry me off to someone. She recruited her boss, Vince, who reluctantly agreed to a marriage of convenience for legal purposes. No date was set, but she was certain this was the way to go, and we would need to implement it soon. I couldn't have cared less what it would take to secure my freedom. As difficult, uncertain, lonely, and scary as life was now, I couldn't fathom returning to my deranged father or entering the dreaded juvenile system.

When I told Lionel about Connie's plan to marry me off to be legally independent, he lit up. "Why don't we get married, Stephanie? Why don't you keep the baby? We can get married and have the baby — our own little family," he appealed. I found myself totally put off by the idea. I knew I was in no position to be a mother, and Lionel was in no way capable of being a good father. A dealer for a dad? It was not the dream I had aspired to live. Barbie's husband Ken was never a pot dealer, and I damn sure didn't want to give birth to a rapist's child. It was out of the question, and I expressed as much to Lionel. He was pissed. So be it.

Lionel's oppressive nature was increasingly irritating to me, as his need to be in charge of everything was becoming unbearable. I seldom felt that his controlling behavior, which he attempted to disguise as caring, was motivated by anything other than an obsessive need to track my every movement and action.

My father relayed during his call that my mother needed to hear from me. Connie gave me their D.C. phone number, and I called her collect from a pay phone as soon as I could. I missed my mom a lot and often worried about her having to deal with my father all alone. My mom's voice sounded sweet on the phone. "Stephanie it's so good to hear your voice. I've missed you, and I hope you're doing okay."

I struggled to keep from bursting into sobs to her. "I'm fine, Mom. Connie is looking into school for me," I lied. I didn't want to worry her. She had enough to manage with my father, and my current cluster of disasters would only add to her stress. I missed her and there were so many unanswered questions. *Did she truly love me? How could she? What had happened?* It was a bittersweet call.

As our days and weeks together moved along, I found Lionel to be exceedingly possessive of me and jealous of anyone's attention toward me. Whenever we were out together, he disliked any other guys looking at me — I couldn't control that. He also kept trying to dominate me and my life. Finally, feeling smothered and trapped, I left him after about six weeks together. He didn't take the news very well. I found his insecurities surfaced even more blatantly as he yelled about me leaving him.

I moved back in with Connie and Elsie. I was thankful to be back with the two women once again. Lionel had become so suffocating. It was sad to let him go, but a major relief as well. I settled back into my routine with the women and resumed my household chores.

22
CHAINS

"I am a biker, I do what I want, when I want, where I want."
- Unknown

On a hot Atlanta night, while down on Peachtree Street, Connie, Elsie, and I were sitting in a booth, enjoying a rare dinner out at a small diner. It was a favorite of the locals for its home cooking, including fried chicken, mac and cheese, and other favorite comfort foods. We heard a group of loud motorcycles roll up and park outside the home-style cafe. Within minutes, I heard Elsie murmur "uh-oh," right about the time this large, bald man covered in leather and metal chains scooted me over in the booth so he could sit right next to me. My eyes shot over to the women, looking for guidance. I read the sense of fear on Elsie's face. She quickly masked it, casually saying, "Hi, Chains, what's up with you these days?" Chains, I would learn, was a member of the Atlanta Outlaws, the local chapter of a national gang. "I'm copasetic. Just cruising the town," he mused. "Who's this chickadee here?"

"Oh, that's Charlotte," she lied.

"I'm watchin' for a ole' lady," he grinned, revealing a flashy gold tooth. "One that's a good lay and loyal."

I suddenly realized what was happening. I'd heard and read enough about motorcycle gangs. He was deciding whether I would leave with him that night. Elsie tried to explain that I was a friend of theirs when I heard a distinct sound that is now deeply embedded in my long-term memory — the opening snap of a switchblade. I followed the sound down to my midriff where Chains held a long, shiny knife. He lifted it ever so slightly and flicked my braless nipples through my shirt. I stared, frozen, watching this blade graze my breasts. Terrified, I took my cue from Elsie to avoid reacting. I sat there, motionless, and silent. Elsie never shut up. She kept talking to Chains in her cool, confident, and casual manner. As the knife flicked my breasts, she carried on, "Chains, we go back how long now? To early Iron Cross days, my friend?"

"Sure enough," Chains grinned widely, flashing his gold tooth again. "I been ridin' a long time."

"Chains, trust me, this one is not the right one for you. She's a family friend, and I'd have fucking hell to pay if you take her. I don't think she'd make a good partner for you, my friend. I know her well enough to know that. Just not your type. It wouldn't be cool fit for you."

I was terrified to make eye contact with Chains. Scarcely shifting the angle of my head, I scanned the diner, looking for anyone who might be watching and able to help if he tried to take me. Several tables registered palpable fear on their faces.

Even if they couldn't see what was happening in our booth, the Outlaws' presence in and around the diner unnerved them. Two guys in a nearby booth could tell what was going on, and their eyes met mine, empathizing with alarm, sorrow, and helplessness. I could only stare back at them in terror.

Suddenly, we could hear the roar of motorcycle engines starting up almost in unison. The thundering sound was deafening as Chains quickly pocketed his knife and left without a word. Apparently, the Outlaws needed to make a swift exit, and it saved me from an awful fate. The entire diner breathed a collective sigh of relief as the gang booked it. Elsie just as easily could have left me to life as a biker's old lady, but she stuck by me that night and protected me the best she could, and I gained a newfound respect for her.

23
SHEILA, MEL, AND MARTIN

"Maybe love at first sight isn't what we think it is. Maybe it's recognizing a soul we loved in a past life and falling in love with them again." - Kamand Kojouri

Sheila lived down the hall, a few doors from Connie's apartment. A slim, plain but pretty girl around 20 years old, she befriended me in the elevator one day that summer and invited me to visit her anytime. It was enjoyable having someone closer to my age to hang out with. I would go to Sheila's apartment and sit around talking with her while she sewed or did chores. I found it fascinating that she was so domestic and also a bit dorky for someone of her age. In time, I came to realize that Sheila was a strong, independent woman, especially for the times. She wasn't a hippie, but a strait-laced and simple city girl, making her way in the world. I admired her tenacity and strength. Our friendship grew as we spent more time together, and I found her inspiring in her own unique way.

"You know, there's a guy living down the hall who is a real pimp," Sheila volunteered one day.

"Seriously? How do you know him?"

"We met in the hallway a while back. You'll probably get to meet him someday, too. His name is Mel. He recruits women to have sex with men who will pay good money for it. I was kind of curious about doing it myself, but he talked me out of it. He said I was too nice of a girl to get mixed up in that dark world." It surprised me that Sheila, so proper and a virtual homebody, would even consider it.

It wasn't long before we ran into Mel in the hall, and after introductions, he invited us to his apartment. He appeared Middle Eastern, tall, with a large frame and dark, wavy hair that surrounded his olive complexion. The prominent nose was telling, as well. He worked his call-girl business into the conversation, mentioning his lucrative porn movies, something I had never heard of. "I need a job so I can make some money," I admitted. "What would it take to be in one of your movies?"

"Well for one thing, you can choose two cities, where the movie won't be sold," he assured me, "so your family or friends won't find out." I believed him, but then he gave me the same spiel he had given Sheila, saying that I was a nice girl who shouldn't take this route in life. Fortunately, I listened.

When I wasn't spending time with Sheila, I would often go to Piedmont Park to hang out. The Allman Brothers, not yet famous, jammed at Piedmont Park on Sundays, and it became one of my favorite jaunts. While dancing to "Revival," one Sunday, I spotted Martin Smith, and as he caught sight of me, his smile grew wider. He sauntered over in baggy jeans and a yellow t-shirt with the Russian sickle on it and promptly asked, "Where's Lionel?"

"We're not together anymore," I said sheepishly.

With a wide grin, he picked me up off my feet, embraced me, twirled me around and around, and laughed as he said softly, "I've been waiting for this day ever since we met."

His charm melted me. I couldn't believe he was so taken with me. For the first time in my life, I felt I had found true love. He made me feel like he recognized and appreciated something special and good within me. Martin didn't have his own place, so we met at the park often and talked endlessly.

I was hesitant to tell Martin about my current predicaments. He was obviously not one to embrace any drama, but I would have to risk telling him the truth. I felt I owed it to him, like I had Lionel.

One Saturday at the park, I broached the subject straight on. "I need to tell you what is happening with me," I hesitated. "I'm pregnant and scheduled to get an abortion in a few weeks by a nurse coming down from Boston."

"Hmmm," Martin began slowly, calmly, with a furrowed brow. "What's the deal? Who's the father? Does he know what's happening?" His foot tapped as he rocked back and forth, drawing deeply on his Camel.

"No," I responded quietly. "He raped me. He's a real asshole. I hope he rots in hell one day. It happened two nights after my father left me. He was at a small party that Connie and Elsie had. They thought he was a cool guy. I thought he was nice enough. Wasn't that way after all." I finished, staring down at my hands.

"That's some pretty heavy shit there," Martin said, processing the news. "You cool with what all has to go down?"

"Yeah," I offered. "I try not to think about it. It happened. It sucks. Now I have to deal with it."

That was the extent of the discussion, thankfully. The burden was challenging enough for me to grapple with on my own. I certainly didn't want it interfering with my first chance at a fairy tale ending in my life's dilemma, and I locked it all back away.

24
THE PROCEDURE

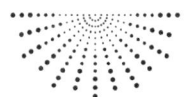

"Things bled. They bled and bled and would not stop bleeding. There would be no dramatic end, she realized, only a slow withering [...] bleeding and more bleeding."
- Richard Flanagan

*L*eona, the nurse from Boston, planned to be in town during the coming week and scheduled a day to perform the abortion. Elsie and Connie were moving from their apartment to a rental house out in the country the same week, so Sheila reluctantly agreed that I could stay at her apartment after the abortion. The day of the procedure, Elsie dropped me off at the house where Leona was staying. The petite redhead with a jutting nose and large brown eyes met me at the front door and ushered me inside. We had the place to ourselves — a quaint house with traditional furnishings and a darkness that permeated the home from a lack of windows and the constant shade of dense trees surrounding the property. The air was heavy with dampness, and a dank odor of stale water was wafting from some unknown source.

We held sparse conversation as Leona led me into a bedroom. "Take off your jeans and leave them on the chair there," she pointed to an old stuffed rocking chair. "Then lie on top of the bed here," she instructed quietly in a thick Boston accent.

Someone had removed a patchwork quilt bedspread from the iron-framed bed and folded it over the rocking chair back. I climbed onto the double bed's center, where a small stack of neatly folded sheets lay. Leona separated my legs and bent them at the knees to simulate a medical table with stirrups. I could see metal instruments, a pot of soapy liquid, sections of plastic tubing, and other medical supplies laid out beside my feet.

Leona inserted a cold metal instrument into my vagina and then a plastic tube. I felt little to nothing — some pinching along with uncomfortable pressure. After a couple of minutes, she took the tube and metal instrument out and announced, "That's it. We're done. You will need to rest for the next couple of days, okay? In the next 24 hours, you will experience some cramping, much like a difficult period would be. The contents of your uterus will be eliminated, and it will all be over soon. Just wear pads until the bleeding stops," she finished. There would be no nifty type-written handout with clear instructions to refer to.

I tried to comprehend it all. I felt desensitized, just going through the motions, almost hovering outside myself, and observing the scene from a distance. "You can get dressed now," she broke my trance. I got up and placed the pad she handed me in my underwear and got dressed. It was all so embarrassing, but what the hell could I do? This was my world now. No sooner than I dressed I heard Leona say, "It looks like Elsie is here to pick you up."

Elsie was indeed outside and waiting to take me back to the apartments. She casually asked how it went, but other than that, there was little conversation. "You should be fine, Steph," she reassured quietly. "As Leona likely told you, you're probably going to experience some cramping and then you'll expel blood clots. It's uncomfortable, but it won't be too much to handle. Just stay as relaxed as you can, and it'll be over before you know it." She explained it like someone who had probably experienced her own abortion or knew intimately of one. "Connie and I will be unpacking at the country house all week, so call us if you need anything," she added.

I arrived at Sheila's, feeling discomfort but nothing unmanageable. Sheila had a one-bedroom apartment and set up her beige sofa pull-out-bed for me in the living room. I lay down and went to sleep. I don't know how long I slept before the cramping woke me. It continued through the night as I bled, and the throbbing spasms intensified. I got into a warm bath, hoping to relieve some of the pain. It was a temporary fix, and the cramping only magnified. In the wee hours of the morning, I started passing large clots of blood. They were so large that I had to pull them out of my body and drop them in the toilet. It continued for hours.

During one episode, I pulled out a larger, firmer clot, only to discover a tiny male fetus. Ten fingers, ten toes, flawlessly formed. He lay motionless in the palm of my hand as I studied him intently. In shock and numb, I told him I loved him and how sorry I was that this had to happen. And I wept. A guttural cry emerged from deep within, wrenched with agony and despair. I couldn't bear the thought of flushing him down the toilet. It was heinous. Feeling myself weakening, I knew I didn't have time to wait any longer before I would pass out. I loosened my hold, giving a slight pull to remove him from the sticky, drying blood, and watched as he slid gently into the toilet. As I saw his tiny body getting flushed away, I sobbed uncontrollably. *What would Daddy think of this? Is this what he wanted for me?*

The bathroom smelled of old pennies and was slippery from the copious amounts of blood everywhere. I did my best to clean it up and tried to get back to the sofa bed, but I blacked out and caught myself on Sheila's curio cabinet. The last thing I remember was the crash as the cabinet and all of its contents fell down around me. I tried unsuccessfully to yell for help when I hit the floor, my voice inaudible.

I don't know how long I lay passed out, bleeding on the floor before I woke up. Crawling to the sofa and pulling myself up was incredibly difficult. I drifted in and out of consciousness, the world around me fading in and out of focus.

Sheila didn't come running when her treasures crashed down with the curio cabinet. Ignoring the sound, she made a choice to distance herself from whatever was unfolding. I got the picture. The guilt of destroying her belongings and the discomfort of bleeding all over her bathroom and sofa bed amplified the misery I found myself in. No amount of pads could contain the volume of blood flowing out of me. The crimson ring around me on the mattress grew as I lay there, bleeding profusely for the next day, crying quietly under the covers as waves of horror overwhelmed me. I struggled to stay awake, and my body temperature fluctuated. I would break out in intense sweating, only to be followed by violent shivering. While Sheila was away at work, two of her friends stopped by, one of whom I knew, Ted Cantrell. Even in the major city, it felt like a small world with its close-knit hippie community. I knew Ted as the brother of my good friend Johnny.

Ted and Ronnie caught sight of the blood-soaked sofa bed, and their horrified expressions said it all. "What the hell happened to you Stephanie?" Ted said in disbelief.

"I had to get an abortion. I'm waiting for the bleeding to stop," I sputtered out almost incoherently. They gaped at the four-foot diameter pool of blood, while the mattress reeked of a moist metallic stench.

"I'm calling Mama," Ted said with urgency and fear. Mama Cantrell was a nurse and mother to six strapping Cantrell boys in Gainesville, Georgia. "Mama," Ted said gravely, "My friend Stephanie's over here bleeding away. She had to have an abortion. Something happened and now she can't stop bleeding. I'm scared for her. There's so much blood everywhere, and I don't know what to do." Mama insisted on talking to me, so he held the phone handset up to my ear.

"Stephanie, you have a massive infection," I could hear her say. There was no judgment in her voice, only kindness and true concern. "If you don't get to a hospital right away, you will bleed to death." She spoke slowly, recognizing my delayed comprehension. "Promise me, Stephanie, that you will get to Grady Hospital right away. They will take care of you. Please do this and don't wait at all. Time is of the essence here."

I rested a moment before asking Ted to dial Connie's number for me. Elsie answered and said Connie wasn't there. I dreaded telling Elsie about the situation, but I had no choice. She was furious about the complications.

"What's happening?" she demanded.

"I don't know," my voice was raspy. It was getting more and more difficult to speak. "I can't stop bleeding, and I'm really weak."

"Did you get into a bathtub or something like that?" she asked.

"Yes. I was in pain. A warm bath," I mumbled out slowly.

"Well, dammit! You shouldn't have done that! I'm sure Leona would've told you NOT to get into a bathtub for fear of infection."

"No, she didn't say anything," I rallied.

"Look, if you go to the hospital, they're going to ask you a million questions about what happened to you. If you say it was an abortion, Leona could be arrested, you get it?!"

"I wouldn't do that. I'll say I had a miscarriage. Promise. I won't say anything about Leona." It was exhausting to talk, but I knew it was imperative, and I pushed myself.

"Well," Elsie conceded. "If you feel you've gotta go to the hospital, sign in under a fake name. You won't be able to remember and react to a new first name, but you can adapt to a new last name. So ... use the name Stephanie but come up with a new last name, got it?"

"Yes," I thought for a moment and first came up with Willingham. "I'll be Stephanie Willingham," I told Elsie. I was drained and just needed approval to go to Grady. Mama Cantrell was so adamant about it, and I trusted her judgement. Satisfied that I understood the gravity of the situation, Elsie relented and said she would let Connie know what was going on. I had to rest before calling Martin.

I got in touch with him by having Ted contact the front desk of the frat house where Martin had temporarily rented a room. They found Martin and got him to the phone. "Martin, something went wrong. I need to go to Grady," I whispered.

"I'll be right there, hang tight," he assured me. He came right over and helped me get dressed and down to a cab waiting at the curb. I slumped against him as we rode toward Grady

Hospital, spent from getting dressed and going down the apartment elevator. Martin wiped the beads of sweat from his brow and explained that he couldn't deal with hospitals and would have to drop me off at the door. I told him what name I would give the hospital in case he wanted to call me.

25
GRADY MEMORIAL HOSPITAL

"Abolition of a woman's right to abortion, when and if she wants it, amounts to compulsory maternity: a form of rape by the State." - Edward Abbey

Walking through one of the Grady Hospital entrances, I was immediately confused. There was a desk, but no apparent waiting room. Three people sat behind the desk. "How can we help you today?" one acknowledged me.

"I'm bleeding from a miscarriage," I answered as quietly as I could and yet still be heard by them. No one was around to overhear, but I was self-conscious and scared, attempting to be discreet.

"You need to take the elevator up to the fourth floor, hon," one woman directed as she pointed over to the wall of elevators to my left.

I exited the elevator on the fourth floor, noticing a nurses' station down the hall, 50 feet to my left. With one step in that direction, I felt myself drift peacefully away and crumple onto the floor, swaying down into a heap. There was no longer enough blood circulating in my body to stay upright. The resulting escape was such a relief. I lost consciousness, knowing I had made it to help.

Struggling to stir myself awake, I felt the bright lights shining on me, heard the whirring of medical equipment, and glimpsed the flurry of hospital personnel running around. Someone was yelling. It took a minute to see the doctor at the end of my operating table, peering at me over my draped legs propped in stirrups. He was screaming, "Who did this to you?! Who did this to you?!"

I mustered the energy to mumble, "I had a miscarriage."

"You are lying! You are lying to me — who did this to you?!" I could feel his wrath clearly directed at me. The nurses bustled around, monitoring all the tubes in me and inserting more. None of them spoke. They performed their tasks dutifully.

I could feel disdain and revulsion. The atmosphere was saturated with dark emotion, a cocktail of antiseptics and icy shoulders. I retreated to a safe place to escape the hostility and bloody chaos.

I woke up sometime that night, lying on a hard, freezing mattress in the ICU. The bitter cold had me shaking uncontrollably, my teeth chattering violently. I was desperately thirsty. Multiple needles with tubes protruded from my body. Blood and clear liquids were being pumped into me. Another tube caught my urine. Beeping machines stood guard, and it took me a bit to comprehend the situation. *OK, I'm in the hospital. I'm so weak. I'm so cold. I'm so thirsty. I can't stop shaking, and all I want is water. Please, some water.*

I tried to get to the sink for water. Before I could even attempt to set a foot on the floor, a nurse was in my room. "You need to lie back down right now. Do not attempt to get up," she insisted.

"But I need some water. Please." I begged in a dry, raspy tone I could barely hear, myself.

"You can't have any water yet. You'll be able to have ice chips soon. Someone will bring them to you in a while," she stated curtly.

"Why's this mattress so cold?" I questioned again in a barely audible hush.

"You're on an ice mattress to reduce your fever. You need to lie there and be still." She was painfully matter-of-fact. So that was that. I sank back into oblivion.

During a lucid moment, I heard two nurses talking in hushed voices outside my cracked-open door. It must have been a shift change. One nurse said to the other, "I'm not sure if this one is going to make it through the night or not." *Was she talking about me?* I lay there in disbelief. *I could die through the night?* Afraid to sleep after that, I feared I would never wake up. I fought sleep as long as I could. I did wake up the next morning, still bleeding, still weak, and pretty damn miserable overall, but I was alive.

I stayed in the hospital for somewhere between one and two weeks, hooked up to bags of fluids and blood. The days dragged on, so it felt like forever. The bare walls in blank rooms reflected my mind-numbing mood. Nurses and doctors took care of my physical needs, but none spoke other than to ask perfunctory medical questions. I was desperately lonely. There was nothing to do but lie there, trapped in my thoughts as the rerun of what happened played on a loop. The record kept spinning. I faced the horror that this was a just consequence of my actions. There was no reason for anyone to show me compassion, considering the chain of events. I was a nuisance to my parents and dispensable. Catholicism sneaked in. *Was God punishing me for the abortion?* Again, I cried during the nights under the cover of a heavily worn hospital blanket. Other times, I would muster a bit of compassion and tell myself, *I'm getting through this fucking hell the best I can.*

The first time I was ever in a hospital flashed into my memory. When I was 3 or 4 years old, I had my tonsils removed at Walter Reed Army Medical Center Hospital in Washington, D.C. I remember lying on the operating room table, the bright lights overhead casting a sterile glow. As I lay there, a red mask loomed closer to my face, its rubbery texture and the faint smell of anesthesia filling my senses. The next thing I knew, I was awake in a crib, and red Jell-O was served, much to my delight. I noticed my mother and father standing out in the hallway looking in at me, and my father waved. I was so excited to see them, I climbed out of the crib and ran toward them, hollering, "Papo, mi papo!" Someone scooped me up and returned me to my crib before I reached them, and I cried at being separated from my parents.

The next time, again at Walter Reed, was for vaccinations to travel overseas. As a five-year-old, I knew all too well that I hated shots, the hot syrupy fluids injected into my arms or butt. They hurt, plus they were downright scary — a needle stabbing your skin like a little knife. When I realized we were there to get shots, I told my mother I needed to go to the bathroom. She let me go to the restroom that was a few feet away. I got into a stall, locked the door, and put my feet up on the toilet. When my mother eventually came looking for me, an ordeal ensued. I refused to come out for her or any of the number of other women now trying to cajole me out of the stall. When all had failed, a smaller woman shimmied under the stall door and unlocked it. I had to get the shots. *I could be quite a little shit when I was a kid.*

That I was too young to die lingered. *People my age died? Absolutely, they do. I knew someone who died even younger.* The recollection surfaced softly. Cautiously. I was eight years old, and the phone rang. It was my best friend Mary's mother, the beautiful Mrs. Wilton. She wanted to know if any of us had seen or heard from Luanne Mesner that day. I barely knew her name. She was two years older than Mary and me. No, we had not. At school the next day, I learned of Luanne's fate. They found her dead at the bottom of the well in their backyard, holding her lifeless kitten. I may not have known her, but her death had a tremendous impact on me. It was a shock — a jolt to my psyche. *She knew the entire way down that well that she was going to die. How horrified was she?*

People speculated her kitten was on the edge of the well, and afraid that it might fall in, she stretched over to grab it and fell, holding her kitten. It was terrifying. I wasn't ready to die. The nurses never told me whether I was getting better. I could only hope that I was.

With too much time to ruminate, dark memories continued to surface. During an argument, my mother complained, "I had two abortions before getting pregnant with you. Sometimes I wish I'd had one with you, too." It stung. I knew I was unlovable, but to that extent? She wished I had never been born to her. She came into my room later that day to apologize. "I'm sorry for saying what I did to you earlier. I was tired, and I honestly didn't mean it," she said wearily. I just listened. What was there to say? I was 14 and worthless, a hippie chick not living up to their expectations. My mother was old and tired. Done with kids, she had no maids to pass off my care to. She resented me and her current situation terribly. As hard as life was for me in those first years back in the States, it was awful for my mother as well. *What were her abortions like? What would she think about my abortion? Did she have complications?*

Eventually, they moved me to a room where a younger doctor, who wasn't attending to me, visited every day. "Do you want to talk about what happened to you?" he asked. I responded by only shaking my head "no." No one had my trust. I convinced myself they all hated me and despised what I'd done. They couldn't know all that I'd been through, or that I was only 15. I knew where they were coming from. Undeterred by my silence, the young doctor came into my room every day during one of his breaks. He would move a chair near the head of my bed and quietly eat his lunch. Despite not discussing the incident, I eventually made small talk with him. Unable to express it at the time, I was grateful for his daily visits. I was desperately lonely and anxious, and his kind, quiet presence helped me feel human. Like someone cared a little. He was the only visitor I had during my lengthy stay at Grady.

Martin called once to check on me. "Hey! How're you doing there? What's been happening?"

"Not much," I answered softly. "I have tubes all over me, and they keep giving me bags of blood." We had a brief chat about what he'd been up to and the nothingness going on for me. I lamented there not being any books for me to read. Martin assured me I'd have plenty to read once I was allowed to go.

"Look, when you're getting discharged from there, find me. I'll come pick you up, okay?" he said pertly. I hung up with a sense of peace, knowing I would be with Martin when I was released. His was the only phone call I received during my stay at Grady. It was a long, lonely stopover.

Filling out the hospital discharge paperwork, I gave my fake name of Stephanie Willingham, 18, and gave Connie's name and phone number as Connie Willingham, my aunt. I registered false addresses and never admitted to an abortion, much less who performed it.

Getting out of the hospital was a challenge. They wanted payment on my substantial bill, and I had no money. I called Connie from the business office and spoke to her as *Aunt Connie*. "Hi, Aunt Connie, it's Stephanie. I'm at Grady Hospital, ready to check out, but they want a payment, and I don't have any money. Can you help me out?"

"Hi, Stephanie," Connie responded. "Let me speak to the office clerk, and I'll try to help you get out of there. Are you doing okay?"

"Yes, I'm fine and all healed now. Can you please find Martin and let him know I need a ride? The best way to reach him is through the front desk at the fraternity house. Here's the lady helping me check out." Connie explained to the discharge clerk that she would send a payment right away, and they let me go. They never got a payment.

Martin arrived in a small, old, borrowed two-seater sports car. I met him outside one of the hospital entrances, and he gave me a big hug and smile as we reunited for the first time in weeks. He brought his good friend Chuck with him, whom I had not met before. I sat in the back jump seat since Chuck was a big guy and could only fit up front.

Martin said we would go to the Morningside Cafe for a healthy dinner as soon as I had a chance to shower and rest.

"Hey, Steph," Martin suggested during our ride, "if you don't want to move out to the country with Connie, you can stay with me for a while. I just need to make sure you understand that I may want to hook up with some other chicks from time to time. You know, for balling, only. I don't want to be tied down to just one lady friend. I need some variety from time to time." It was crushing. Demoralized couldn't touch what I was feeling and experiencing.

Even Chuck commented, "Dude, you sound so cold. That was harsh, man. She's just getting out of the hospital, too."

Again, I fought back tears as I stared out the window. *I am obviously not worthy. I am not enough.* Unable to respond, I fell silent as we headed over to the frat house room Martin was subleasing at Georgia Tech University during the summer break. It was a tiny room, with a bunk bed on top with a desk and chair underneath. When we arrived, I climbed up to the bunk and escaped into slumber. I was so relieved to be out of the hospital and on the road to recovery — both physically and mentally.

26
MARTIN STERLING SMITH, JR

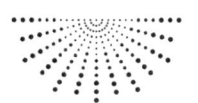

"Trouble is the common denominator of living. It is the great equalizer." - Soren Kierkegaard

Martin was 22, seven years my senior, and I looked up to, loved and admired him. Scholarly and knowledgeable, he had the intellect of my father, but was cool, a perfect fit for me. At 6'2", he was slender with an athletic build and haunting blue eyes. His blondish hair delicately framed his beautiful facial features.

Martin introduced me to Buddhism, Hinduism, Astrology, Tarot, Montessori education, nutrition, vegetarian eating, the value of staying fit, the love of reading and listening to music, consistently learning, and experiencing anything new. The list was endless. That Martin came into my life at this malleable age was a stroke of good fortune. His positive attitude and outlook were what I needed, along with his loving spirit. Also extremely smart, I would one day learn his IQ had tested as high as 165. I may not have been in a traditional school, but Martin made sure I was learning continuously. We spent our free time reading voraciously. The local cafes and friends kept us stocked and stoked.

I was not aware, however, of his challenges with addiction. I only knew he smoked pot. Police arrested him a few months ago at Piedmont Park, and his trial was approaching. "I borrowed money from my younger brother Daniel to score some reefer, since he had cash from his student loans. He was in college until this shit went down. I cop to being the reason he's not there anymore. I scored 12 pounds of some solid Acapulco Gold buds that I knew would sell out fast. The plan was to have Daniel's money back to him with some profit in a matter of days."

His retelling of that fateful day intrigued me. "I took the load over to the park to sell on a Sunday — the best dealing day because freaks want to get their stash worked out for the coming week. I parked Daniel's car and set out to walk the crowds and get a vibe for what was going on and what was being sought after. Before long, I was hip to cops busting their way through the park, and I headed back to the car to leave. When I reached Daniel's MG, the cops were already at the back, getting ready to pop the trunk. I turned around and headed the other way when a cop yelled out to me, 'STOP!' I knew I was busted, so I took my chances and booked it."

"The cops chased me. I ran across Piedmont Avenue and into one of those apartments across the street from the park.

One was open, so I went in and ran upstairs and through to a window that led to the roof. I had a friend that used to live in those, so I knew the layout." He paused briefly before continuing in a lower voice. "As I jumped out onto the tile roof, I tripped and fell. The pigs caught up with me by then and proceeded to beat the shit out of me. Their batons tore up my back and sent me into crushing pain. They didn't let up for several minutes, and it seriously fucked me up. When they finally stopped, I could hardly move. They jerked me up onto my feet with hands behind my back, slapped handcuffs on me, and shoved me into the paddy wagon. I sat back there with other locals getting busted along with me. Possession with intent to sell, a charge guaranteed to score you time in lockup," he concluded.

Thinking his brother Daniel must have bailed him out, I only knew that he had a lawyer and would go to court for this arrest soon. I was worried I would lose him to prison in the coming months. We smoked pot every day, and Martin was still selling weed to make money.

When the fall semester began, we had to move out of the frat house. With nowhere to go, we started an endless shuffle from one friend's apartment to the next. One pretty trashy place was a bit more than I could stand. The messy, dirty room offered only a nasty mattress on the filthy floor. The rumpled sheets were old, torn, soiled, dingy and reeked of spoiled trash. I slept on top of them, afraid of what I'd find between or under them. I wasn't wrong. We caught crabs that entailed a trip to the free clinic, including solutions to apply. It was painstakingly gross.

At another house we were crashing at, I walked into the bathroom to find Martin unresponsive, in a stupor, with a needle hanging out of his arm. He was catatonic. I screamed in panic. His friend came rushing in, pulled the needle out of his arm and helped get Martin to the bed, where he had a seizure of some sort. Even with his eyes open, it was clear from his vacant stare that he could not see or hear. Beside him, I lay paralyzed by anxiety, dreading his life slipping away right next to me.

"Hey, he's gonna be alright. He's just kinda OD'd some with this smak. It's pretty good shit and he's gonna be trippin' big time, but he'll be fine, don't worry. Just stay here by him and make sure he doesn't go all in. He'll be back soon, believe me," his buddy drawled on. I hated this piece of shit.

Why did he give Martin heroin? And why did Martin even take it? I was confused and really pissed off. It seemed like forever before Martin came back to. He was disoriented and high. I was sick. I did not know he ever even tried heroin. Once he sobered up, I burst into tears of relief and pleaded with him never to do this again. He promised he wouldn't. I think the episode scared him into reality. Thankfully, he never shot up smak again, to my knowledge. I knew then I would never stay with someone who shot up drugs. Not my thing, ever.

We continued from one friend's pad to another. A few times when we couldn't find a place to stay, we'd just set up pallets to sleep on, hidden in the park. We could fit everything we owned into our two Army backpacks we stole from the Army Surplus store.

In the fall of 1971, Martin ended up back in jail. He appeared in court for a scheduled hearing, only to discover that the date had been moved up and he had missed it. Reaching him was nearly impossible with no home or phone of his own. They booked him then and there and threw him in jail. He needed $150 to bail out, so I went to his brother Daniel, but he refused to spend any more of his meager money on his brother. He had been burned too many times. Helpless, desperate to get Martin out of jail, I had absolutely no money and panhandled just to afford phone calls to Martin's lawyer and a meal each day.

27
CALLING MEL

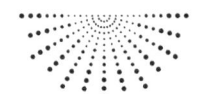

∼

"She didn't have a soul to sell." - S. Pleasant

∼

Utterly desperate, I remembered about Mel and his business. I got his number from Sheila and bummed enough change to call him from a pay phone. "Mel, it's Stephanie who used to live down the hall," I said.

"Hi Stephanie, how've you been?" he chimed in.

"To be honest, I'm not doing okay right now," I said, my voice trembling with vulnerability. "My boyfriend, Martin, is locked up because he missed his court date that got changed on him. I need to come up with $150 for his bail — quickly, like in the next day. I really need to do some work for you. Can you set me up with something?" I pled.

Mel must have sensed my despair and heard the anguish in

my voice. I expected him to talk me out of it again, but he confirmed with me, only once, "You sure you want to do this, Steph?"

"Yes. I have to, Mel. There's really no choice," I answered flatly. "I have no other way to make this money."

"Well, let me see what I can find for you. Call me back in about two hours, okay? I think I already have someone in mind, let me just confirm it, okay?" He sounded optimistic. Right at two hours, I called Mel back.

"Steph, the person I was thinking of is a recently divorced business man that only wants some company for a while and a blowjob. You'll be safe with him, and he lives in an upscale apartment complex with another guy. It's $50. Collect it from him as soon as you get to his place. Don't perform any services until he has paid you. Got it?"

"Uh-huh," I replied, relieved for the coming money, and ignoring what it required.

"It's at 2:00 p.m. tomorrow. Where do you want him to pick you up?"

Without enough time to weigh what I was preparing to do and how it would affect me for decades to come, I was on a mission to get Martin out of jail, and that's all I focused on. I agreed to the specified time and gave him an address on Spring Street to pick me up from Daniel's rental house.

Mel also knew I needed to make more than that $50, so he offered himself as a client. He picked me up later that day and took me to a cheap roadside motel. He said he needed to know I could give a blowjob and have sex, so I would need to practice on him. Disgusted, anguish took command and consumed my psyche. He was so large I could barely get a little more than the head of his penis in my mouth. Satisfied I could give a blow job, he paid me $50 and said I was ready for tomorrow's arrangement, thankfully without having sex with me.

I waited by the street for my "client." All I knew about him was that he was a recently divorced business executive and lonely. Amazingly, when Mel told the man I was only 15, he said he couldn't ask me for "services," and would just like me to keep him company for the afternoon — that he would still pay the $50. I was beyond relieved and thrilled. I knew from my encounter with David, horrific as it played out, that I could pull off an adult conversation with someone older than me. This meeting with the divorcee should be doable with minimal anxiety and shame. At the designated spot on Spring Street, he pulled his car over, greeted me, and leaned across the seat to open the passenger door. "Are you Stephanie?" he asked as I got into his car. He was a typical businessman in his late 30s or early 40s. Short, a little pudgy in the middle, well dressed in khakis and a blue button-down shirt, with sparse, acutely coifed hair and dark-rimmed thick glasses. He was on the nerdy side, a corporate geek, and his name was Don.

Don rented an apartment at a lavish, expensive complex in the Buckhead area with a roommate. The apartment was immaculate and had sleek lines and modern furniture. I chatted it up with Don, relieved that I only had to keep him company for an afternoon. I sat on the plush beige carpet with my back against the black leather sofa in his living room. "Hey, my roommate may be coming back here soon. If you don't mind, I'd like to keep our personal arrangement private. He doesn't need to know about it."

"No, I don't mind," I answered honestly. I didn't care who his roommate was or what he thought. It didn't concern him.

It surprised me when this corporate geek pulled out a bong and started smoking it. Naively, I thought only hippies smoked weed. We were well into a second bowl when he let me know it was laced with speed. I could handle some speed and thought it would help me be more friendly. I was socially awkward with older people, so I welcomed anything to help me fit in better. The geek was rather boring and could use some speed to prompt conversations beyond weather and cityscapes. We progressed in talking about the advantages of growing up and living overseas. I could contribute to that topic.

When his roommate did arrive home, Don introduced me as his friend, and I offered a cheerful hello. The roommate seemed a little dumbfounded, raising an eyebrow, but returned the perfunctory hellos and went on with his business. Don picked up the bong and moved us to his bedroom to continue our visit in private.

He divulged nothing about his personal life. I could discern little of his story beyond what Mel had already shared. I sensed he was feeling like a failure. Divorce was still not common, and the stigma attached to it was a life sentence. He seemed ashamed of the breakup of his marriage. My meeting with him was likely meant to provide more than just a sexual encounter. Unfortunately for Don, I didn't have the skills to comfort him or boost his damaged self-esteem.

Several bowls later, Don blurted out, "I feel you are way beyond your years. You seem so much older, so much more mature than your age." He didn't mention my only being 15. Instantly, I resented him and the whole situation as I sensed what was coming.

"Let's revert back to our original agreement of $50 for a blow job," he stated matter-of-factly. I sunk. I cringed. I couldn't believe I was now in a situation where I would be engaging in sexual activity with this old geek. Following Mel's strict rule of collecting money upfront, I already had the $50. I found myself mentally checked out as I went down on him. As if that wasn't bad enough, he then decided he wanted to have sex with me, too. I lay there on the carpeted floor, not even trying to pretend I was enjoying it. Repulsed, the entire process revolted me. He seemed so old; it was disgusting. When he was done, Don took me back to where Daniel and Tom were. There was no conversation until I had him drop me off across the street from the rental house. He tossed me an extra $50, which I promptly grasped in my sweaty and quivering hands.

"Can I see you again sometime?" He asked in all sincerity.

"No. That won't be happening," I answered sarcastically, pissing him off as he slammed the door and screeched away. Flushed and weak, I leaned against a telephone pole and violently puked on the side of busy Spring Street. My body rejected the incident at a core level. I was so pissed and distressed that when I walked into the living room finding Daniel and Tom, I sneered, "I hope you're happy. I just sold myself to get the money for Martin's bail."

Neither spoke a word. They looked down at the shag rug, forlorn. I fought back the tears of shame, begging to burst out of me. Some crept by and down my pale, still clammy face. We sat in silence as the Moody Blues sang *Nights in White Satin* in the background. The experience left me numb and jaded. It destroyed what remaining self-esteem I had lurking inside.

I took the bail money to Martin's lawyer, and he was released the following day. I got to see him for the first time in days when he met me at Tom's apartment, where we would be crashing for a few days. Elated, I was so relieved. I was also proud of myself for coming up with the money, even if it was through miserable means. Martin was worth it to me. He was all I had in this tiny world of mine.

Martin cleaned up and shaved in the bathroom while I sat

on the closed toilet. "How'd you get the bank to pay my bail?" he asked. "Did Daniel get it to you?"

Stammering, buying time to think of how to break the truth to him, I muttered with my head bent down. "I sold myself. I went to that guy, Mel, I told you about a while back and he connected me with a guy who wanted services." Without saying a word, Martin left the bathroom, picked up a softball bat of Tom's and went outside to where his brother Daniel was. I followed quickly, afraid of what was about to happen. Martin started beating Daniel on his back with the bat. Horrified, Tom and I began screaming for him to stop. Despite his attempt to defend me, I couldn't find any satisfaction in his macho behavior because it contradicted my tolerance of violence toward another. He finally stopped as Tom pulled on him, but not before Daniel was seriously doubled over in pain and severely injured. It was repulsive. Appalled as I was, guilt consumed me. It was all my fault. Why couldn't I have just come up with a good lie to tell him?

We never spoke of this grisly time again. By now, I had become quite competent in compartmentalizing hurtful feelings or injurious events. I effectively blocked and locked the memories away. I couldn't afford the luxury of experiencing or giving time to my feelings. My energies focused on staying alive and safe.

28
WE LAND IN A TRAILER

"If you get the chance to give her anything, give her a place to lay her head." - Matt Baker

Martin dealt enough pot to get us a month's rent at an old house on a dead-end street that backed up to Lenox Square Mall. I went to work for a second time in as many months as a hostess at the Lenox Red Lobster restaurant, using my Air Force ID card as identification (it had my father's social security number). Since Martin was usually out driving his old Saab, which he had bought using the money he made from selling pot, I repeatedly had to rely on taking a cab to work and back, which often wiped out whatever money I made during my shift. I enjoyed my job despite some stressful times when people would get impatient and rude as their wait times stretched on. At least it was better and lasted longer than the previous job I had attempted.

Martin insisted I work to contribute financially and not be a burden to him. Never mind that I was too young to drive and didn't have a social security card. He had seen a "help wanted" sign at a head shop on 10th Street, near the corner where it intersected with Peachtree — the same corner where I had a premonition about the car wreck a few short months ago. Too bad my intuition lay dormant as I started my new job.

The head shop, which sold paraphernalia for pot but ostensibly for tobacco, was owned and operated by Mack, a local hippie entrepreneur. Mack hired me right away and had me come in that Friday evening for my first shift as a sales clerk. I stocked the shelves full of goods, kept the store neat, assisted shoppers, and rang up sales. The store sold cool clothes, and Mack had me wear some on my first shift. I changed into yellow satin hot pants and a flowy silk top and gathered inventory in the back. Within minutes, Mack pressed himself against me from behind. I felt his large, firm, upright penis pushing into the crack of my ass. I turned around and walked to the front without saying a word, rattled and anxious. Soon I saw Martin walk by, and I left the store to catch up with him. I told him about Mack humping me in the back of the store, and he told me to get my stuff and leave. With no notice or goodbye, I grabbed my clothes and cigarettes and headed out the door, still wearing the satin hot pants and silk shirt. Martin and I went to the pizza joint at the corner and walked in to a new Rolling Stones song playing over the sound system — *Brown Sugar*. So à propos.

Our rental house enchanted me. They fitted it for wheelchair use, including wide hallways and railed, raised toilets. It was a place of our own. No more panhandling for food money. No more hiding in the park to camp out for a night. No more crab-infested mattresses.

Living right next to the Lenox Square mall, I often walked over there and browsed the stores, yearning for some decent clothes to wear. Eventually, I began shoplifting clothes from the Davidson's store. It was so easy. No one was ever around the teen and ladies' departments where I rifled through the clothes. I took several pieces into the unattended dressing room, and whichever items I wanted to keep, I would stuff down my pants and up under my shirt. My winter coat was an Air Force flight suit we stole from the Army Navy Surplus Store, and it worked magic on hiding anything I wanted to carry out. There were no security tags in those days, so it made for an easy lift. I felt guilty for stealing, but not bad about who I was stealing from. Corporate America was the pigs of the day, along with racist, violent police.

"If you ever get caught stealing, don't you dare call me to come bail you out," Martin admonished me. It hurt my feelings, considering what I had gone through to get him out of jail just a few short months ago. He was adamantly against my shoplifting. I ignored him. It was too easy, and no one ever saw a thing. I had nothing. What the fuck did I have to lose? By sheer luck, I was never caught.

As 1972 rolled in, Martin found an actual job. He became a land surveyor with a guy named Hoke Benton in the suburban Atlanta areas of Marietta and Woodstock. He found a mobile home strip in the Woodstock community, and we rented and moved into an old, dilapidated single-wide trailer with two bedrooms. I decorated our old trailer the best I could with anything I found cheap, free, or out in nature. I made it as comfortable as possible with no money to spend on it. Seeing mismatched decorations and repurposed treasures brought a sense of charm to the humble single-wide. The trailer came furnished with an old, beat-up, and torn sofa. I made a coffee table from overturned milk crates I got from the downtown food co-op. Two used candles from a yard sale sat on top. I always made an altar area of some sort wherever we landed, and this was it for the trailer. I lit candles every night to create an atmosphere.

After leaving my hostess job, Hoke hired me as an assistant for Martin. There was a transit man and a plumb bob holder, and I held the plumb bob steady while Martin got angle readings from the transit machine. Spending my days with Martin in the woods gave me a sense of belonging. We ended up with chigger bites, sometimes hundreds of them, but it was worthwhile to work outside in nature. I also learned how to use a machete to clear paths in the woods from one marking pin to the next.

Hoke won the bid for a big job in Woodstock, and we dedicated weeks to surveying a tract of land that would be divided up into home lots. We met other workers, including Butch, an older man who graded the land. "Do you want to hop up here and take a ride on my grader?" Butch asked me. Fascinated by the enormous machine, I grabbed a pipe to hoist myself up as Butch yelled loudly, "Don't touch that pipe! It'll burn your ass big time!" It was too late. My hand was scorched. Butch jumped down and ran to help, yelling to Martin, "Stephanie's burned her hand, and I'm going to take her to the trailer for ice!"

We got to the trailer, and no sooner than I had ice on my hand, the old bastard pinned me to a wall and forced a kiss on my lips. Disgusted, I yelled, "What are you doing?!" He smiled back at me with amusement. It was yet another unwanted advance from a man, and he revolted me. I rushed back outside before he could try anything else. Yet again, I felt violated and vulnerable. I didn't tell Martin. I was afraid of what might happen if he knew.

Hoke could be a troublesome person to work for, and over time, a deep resentment took root within me. The sight of his condescending gaze and the feelings of his belittling words towards Martin and me became unbearable. At the end of one long, hot workday, Hoke started in on Martin, blaming him for the job taking too long. "What the hell is wrong with you Martin, that this job is taking so long to finish? You're being a lazy ass out there and I've had it with you! I have people to answer to and they're getting frustrated at the long wait. You're doing a piss poor job!" Before Martin could explain, Hoke kept on, "It's not like it's a hard job to do. It's lots for a small strip center."

Impulsively, I took a step forward, retracted my arm, and punched Hoke in the eye. No one treats someone I love like that. I stunned myself as much as I did him. It was too late to take it back. I doubled down and yelled back at Hoke, "You damn asshole! If you would listen to Martin for the real reason this job is taking so long — the property pins aren't marked right, and we have to find them. Not only that, but the woods are also so thick it takes forever to chop through the brush!"

Hoke backed off and carefully replied, "I didn't think you took me so seriously." I turned on my heels and headed to our car, with an elated Martin close behind. He laughed all the way home about the episode. I don't know how, but we didn't lose our jobs that day, and Hoke treated us better after the fateful encounter.

The whole fracas reminded me of the time I hit Guy Cortez in third grade. Guy was pitching the ball in a game of kickball, and I taunted him as I walked up to kick next. "Come on fatso, throw the ball!" I hollered. Guy came running toward me, arms flailing, and landed a hit on me, so I hit him back. I deserved that, and I knew it. The tumbling fight that followed landed us both in the principal's office. There, we received a long lecture on getting along, and we were told to make amends. I was a bully that day, a role I realized I did not revel in.

Martin had given up hard drugs and only smoked pot or drank alcohol. The drinking got worse in those days. He traded one addiction for another. It became worrisome, to say the least. On one occasion, Martin's tormented groans echoed through the sparse bedroom. With each draw, the light from the end of his cigarette highlighted the beads of sweat glistening on his forehead. The weight of his anguish filled the small space, leaving an unsettling feeling of deep fear in the pit of my stomach. By morning, he couldn't bear it any longer, so he went to the local hospital, where they diagnosed him with gastroenteritis and prescribed medication. Although he admitted it was due to too much alcohol, he didn't slow his drinking. He only progressed.

We didn't have any friends to speak of in the Woodstock area, but there was one older couple that we would sometimes visit for company and a filling home-cooked meal.

Bob worked for Hoke as a draftsman, and Martin got to know him through work. He was a likable older guy who was in his fourth marriage. His wife, Frannie, enjoyed drinking as much as he did, and their union seemed to be based solely on their shared love of Jack Daniels.

Frannie was a true Southern cook, and the pair often invited us over to their decrepit, overrun trailer for a meal, and of course, drinking. I didn't drink alcohol, so I was always the only sober one. The meals were indeed fulfilling, but the entertainment provided by Frannie was most engrossing — like a car wreck you couldn't turn away from.

Once sufficiently soused, Frannie would launch into cussing rants that could be heard throughout the trailer park — especially since with no air conditioning, everyone's windows were open during most of the year, and Frannie's mouth could be heard over dinner tables from end to end.

"What da hell ya lookin at, youse son o' bitch?" she'd holler at Bob's face for no obvious reason. Bob knew better than to even respond, as did we. "Youse think I'm ugly ya bastard? Don't youse look at me funny youse stupid fuckin' cunt!," she'd carry on, all the while continuing to cook whatever was on the menu for our dinner. "Fuck all o' ya fucking bastards out thar in them trailers! All's y'all are assholes ya know ya are! Don't ever come knockin' on my door ya git it fuck faces?" she'd yell out the closest open window. "I'll fuck ya up but good ya sorry bastards!" she'd bellow with all the might her wrinkled up, skinny body with the bloated belly could muster. Her thin red hair, wild and unkempt, darted wildly in the air in unison with her gyrations.

By this time, someone outside would have heard her, and if they happened to be drinking too, which they often were, they would engage her in a cussing war. Frannie would win. Her brazenness was as foul as the three-day-old shrimp in their overflowing trash can.

Once dinner was ready, Frannie would quiet down long enough to serve up our plates and sit to eat the meal with us. Actually, though, she just pushed food around her plate while mumbling obscenities. A true alcoholic, she rarely had room for nutrition. She was a great example of why I never wanted to be a drinker. The sight of her stumbling and swaying, her face flushed and her eyes glazed, was a stark reminder of the consequences of over-drinking. Her slurred speech and the clanging of empty bottles only amplified the chaos alcohol had brought into her life. The pungent smell of whiskey emanating from her breath and clothes filled the air, leaving a bitter and stifling aroma. Our friendship with Bob and Frannie may have been short-lived, but the lessons and memories lasted a lifetime.

29
SWEET SIXTEEN

"Live by design, not by accident." - Jan Michael Gaynor

We were still living in the trailer out in Woodstock, when my 16th birthday approached in March 1972. We were dirt poor, so I didn't expect to get anything. I was okay with that, because I was with someone that I loved. He loved me and I felt he was loyal to me, and that was enough. The night before my birthday, Martin came home to the trailer, already pretty wasted. He had been out but never said where. Despite his staggering, he was able to hide the car keys. I didn't know why, but a hunch told me he might have stashed a birthday surprise in the car. I couldn't imagine what it might be and let curiosity get the better of me. Among the childhood stories I shared with Martin was one about hiding all of my Christmas presents in the downstairs guest bathroom. I couldn't resist the temptation to unwrap each one, wanting to see what surprises awaited me. I could expertly unwrap and re-wrap gifts like a pro. After all, I was my mom's gift wrapper every holiday season. Considering that he knew this about me, I wasn't surprised that Martin was trying to hide my birthday gift. He drank some more whiskey and stumbled his way back to our bedroom and passed out. Here was my chance. I retrieved the car keys from the stacked rolls of electrical tape where he had dropped them. Tip-toeing outside, I opened the trunk of our car to find a huge cardboard sign that read: "HA-HA caught you peeking!" I felt utterly humiliated. He had set me up! It was a good one, though, and it taught me a valuable lesson about appreciating delayed gratification.

The next morning, I didn't let on that I had peeked, but somehow Martin knew and got a good laugh out of it. He said we were doing something special for my 16th birthday that involved a two-hour car ride and dressing in jeans and a shirt. I was dying to know what he was up to and where we were going, but he wouldn't give me a hint.

After about an hour and a half ride, Martin pulled the car over, took off his head bandana and wrapped it comfortably, yet snugly, around my eyes. I could feel myself getting excited. This was so off-base. We drove on dirt and gravel roads and finally came to a stop. As Martin took off the bandana, I looked around to see a field of small airplanes everywhere.

"Are we going on an airplane ride?" I exclaimed.

"Nope," he responded. "You're going skydiving!"

My breathing got raspy, my body tensed, and I looked around uneasily. *Jump out of an airplane?* "Are you serious? I don't really want to do this. I'd rather YOU do this and let me watch," I pled with him.

"No way, man," he responded. "This is YOUR birthday present, and it is as unique and rare as you are. This will be an adventure that you will never forget. It's your 16th birthday! It will change you. Besides, I hustled heavy for the stash to buy this for you!"

"No," I continued to plead with him, the anxiety migrating throughout me by now. "This is too scary for me. I really don't want to do it. YOU do it. You'll love it and I'll watch you!" We went back and forth for at least 15 minutes. He refused to give in to me.

"You will have this incredible experience and the story that goes with it. Imagine getting to tell your grandchildren one day that you jumped from an airplane and dove to the ground with nothing but a parachute and some bravery." He finally sold me. I knew there was no way I could out-argue him, so I might as well cave to his enthusiasm. "They don't know you're turning 16," he finally mentioned. "I told them you were turning 18, so you'd be of legal age to do this." The subject never came up. No one even asked me for an I.D.

After four hours of practicing jumps from atop bales of hay and dropping and rolling onto our shoulders, we were ready to jump. There were six other jumpers in my group — all men in their 20s and 30s. I was by far the youngest and lightest, only 105 pounds, soaking wet. Because of my stature within the group, I would be the first jumper out of the aircraft.

I was placed by the plane door, which had a double-latch system that happened not to work. The pilot assured me that the single latch would hold fine, but that if I could hold it in the double-latched position, it wouldn't rattle as loudly the entire way. I could feel the cold metal of the door handle in my fingers, my grip tight. With every fiber of my being, I was determined to prevent anyone from falling out into the vast expanse below. The weight of responsibility pressed upon me, making my palms sweat. It was a daunting task, one that I approached with due reverence.

"Once the door is open, place your left leg on the plane's rudder as you grab the crossbar with your left hand and swing your right leg and foot out to the rudder, your hands hanging on to the cross bar. Let go," reiterated our instructor. "Count to eight and look up to make sure your chute has deployed from the static line and is above your head. If it's not, prepare to deploy your spare chute."

Luckily, my chute was fine, and I was, too. The force of the wind hit my body and threw me into a backwards arch that an army of horses couldn't bring upright. Once I was flung into an upright position with my parachute safely above me, I drifted in the atmosphere of 12,000 feet, where only clouds lived, and entered an altered state. The lack of noise left me feeling deaf. It was magic. I laughed out loud, uncontrollably, giddy beyond measure. The air was thin and pure. Below, the panorama looked like tiny villages in blocks of green, beige, and brown. This was the stuff of mind-blowing adventures, a sensory feast that stirred the soul. At some point, I became aware of voices yelling. Looking down to see where the voices were coming from, I realized there were dozens of people screaming up at me. Finally, I distinguished what they were yelling. "Turn your chute! Pull your toggles to turn your chute! Turn your chute!" They kept yelling until I followed their directions. In my excitement, I had completely forgotten to turn my chute against the wind for the landing. Thankfully, I was able to get it done before the 100-foot dead zone.

I landed on the ground, bending my knees and standing up instead of rolling. I landed second to last, ahead of my instructor, who left the airplane after all seven jumpers successfully exited. He tried to toggle his way into the bullseye target to make a perfect landing, but tilting his chute below the 100-foot mark caused too much air to escape, and he suffered a hard landing and broke his ankle. You could hear his screams. They hauled him to a hospital in a pickup truck, but before they made it out of the lot, he looked out the window at me and said, "You did great Stephanie, you did great! I'm so proud of you!" I was both elated at having accomplished this feat and disturbed about his broken ankle.

30
A MARRIAGE OF CONVENIENCE

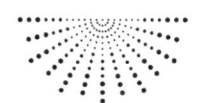

"You always have two choices: your commitment versus your fear." - Sammy Davis, Jr.

Martin's father, Martin, Sr., a commercial apple farmer in central Georgia, wielded some influential political connections in Atlanta. Tree Top Apple Juice bought his apples — one of the most popular apple juices of the day. This alone earned him some clout with the Mayor of Atlanta and others in local government. He brokered a deal in which Martin would voluntarily enter the Army in exchange for his marijuana charges being dropped. Although Martin was not Army material, if he could avoid prison, it would be worth it. Martin hated the armed services and anything related to wars. He rejected the offer of an appointment at West Point after high school. Now, he would have to go into the service as an enlisted man in the Army. Although he criticized the armed services, he respected the commitment he had made, and he knew well that the arrangement had been devised for his benefit. Serving time in the Army would be far better than serving it in a prison somewhere.

One hurdle we had yet to cross was getting married. Martin had an aversion to the traditional institution of marriage. Despite all his pronouncements about never wanting to be tied down by marriage, he wanted me to follow wherever he was stationed. That would require us to get legally married. I got in touch with Connie. "Hey, thought I'd call you with some good news. I need to get married to Martin Smith."

"Wow," Connie said excitedly. "You know, Vince ended up backing out completely. So, this is great news. How'd this come about?" she inquired.

"Martin's father worked out a deal where Martin has to go into the Army for two years and in exchange, his pot dealing charges will be dropped. But, if he gets stationed somewhere overseas, which is likely, we have to be married for me to go with him. So, we need to get married. Martin is a little freaked out about it, but we're just going to go through the motions without anything special."

"Ok, cool," Connie sounded relieved. "We're still living at the house out in the country. Come by there this weekend and I'll have the parental permission forms ready for you to sign. You'll need to go to Walhalla, South Carolina, which is northeast of here and right across the border. Interstate 85 will get you close to there, then follow the signs to Walhalla. There, you can easily get married by a Justice of the Peace or local Probate Judge, with permission forms from a parent."

Martin drove me to Connie and Elsie's country house so we

could pick up the paperwork for our upcoming marriage. Connie was a notary public. She got the proper forms and had me sign my mother's name, which she then notarized. While seeing Connie, I decided I should pick up the rest of my stuff. I had left my suitcase in their care, with my precious jewelry box, including the 24k gold aquamarine ring my parents had given me for my 13th birthday. It was my March birthstone from the beautiful gems mined in Brazil. It was gone. All of my track ribbons; the ribbons our shepherd, Gina, had won in our school pet contests every year (one for being the funniest dog, smiling, as she would drop her lips while upside down and show all her teeth); my first real watch; ribbons for scholastic and athletic awards I had won in school. All gone, not to be seen, touched, or pondered over ever again. I was crushed. The last remnants of my personal history vanished like a lost dream.

Elsie let me know Connie had taken in another teen for a few weeks, who had to use some of my clothes. Apparently, she took off with all of my belongings. Distraught, I tried not to show my heartbreak, as I owed Connie and Elsie so much; I didn't dare complain about the loss of my meager possessions.

Papers signed, Martin and I drove to Walhalla, South Carolina, to a probate judge's office on a sunny Saturday afternoon. Sitting behind his opulent antique desk, he married us on September 23, 1972. An affable older man with wire-rimmed glasses, he was wearing only socks on his feet. He delighted in sharing stories with us about the many odd marriages he had officiated. The strangest one, I thought, was the couple who insisted on getting married on a swimming pool diving board. Martin stayed composed, despite swinging his crossed leg and chain smoking. I figured we could smoke a joint as soon as we were back in the Saab and returning to our trailer.

I wore jeans and a t-shirt, as did Martin. We didn't exchange rings. It was as uneventful as you could make a marriage ceremony, and it helped make the prospect less terrifying for Martin, as well. On the way home, we took a break at a truck stop for dinner. That was the extent of our marriage celebration. We both ordered vegetable plates.

31
AS PATHS CROSS

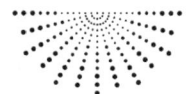

"Life is about not knowing, having to change, taking the moment and making the best of it, without knowing what's going to happen next." - Gilda Radner

At Christmastime, we went to Martin's parents' house in Gay, Georgia. Martin would leave from there to go to boot camp in Columbia, South Carolina, and I would stay with his parents and his little brother Aaron, 13.

Martin told everyone I was 18 to avoid any legal or personal questions, and this included his family. The pressure was on trying to act older than I actually was. Thankfully, I loved his family, especially Martin Sr., who was always exceedingly kind to me.

Although sad when Martin left, I knew we would be

together again in the coming months. Once again, I made the best of my situation, a new life with his family. I was so fond of his brother, Aaron. He did not know I was only three years older than him. We planted strawberries, picked cotton, and turned the farm chores into adventures. Aaron also taught me how to drive a car. We almost got into trouble several times, but survived it all. After getting my driver's license, I took my first road trip to South Carolina to visit Martin at boot camp. Having not yet mastered taking off on a hill from a stopped position with a clutch, I ran two red lights on hills in our old Saab. It was that or roll backward into another car. C'est la vie.

By winter of 1973, Martin was in his newly stationed post, Ansbach, West Germany. I would join him as soon as he found us an apartment to rent. It seemed to take forever, but eventually we had a time frame. I would move there in June.

When Phil, as they called my mother-in-law, found out my parents didn't know I was married, she prodded me to contact them.

"Your parents would want to know your good news, Stephanie. You should call them. Please use my bedroom phone for privacy," she offered. Alas, I knew I needed to face the dreaded phone call and contact my parents. I thought they would freak out, but instead, I immediately sensed great relief on their part as they each listened on separate phone extensions.

"Oh, how wonderful, Stephanie, what's your new last name now?" My mother asked right away.

"It's Smith," I let her know.

"You don't mean that Bobby Smith, do you?" she asked, fear quaking in her voice. I bristled at her comment, remembering how awful they had treated Bobby.

"No, mother, it's Martin Smith. He's amazingly smart, and

he's in the Army. He is stationed with an artillery unit in Ansbach, West Germany. I'll be joining him there this winter or spring as soon as he finds us an apartment."

"That all sounds good, Steppa," my father chimed in. I was unaware that he was listening in on another phone extension. He, too, sounded relieved.

There it was. They were finally free of me and any responsibility. I finally got it. Their consciences were clear. No more guilt. No more shame for leaving me. "Stephanie has run off and gotten married," would be their new story. As usual, my mother didn't probe, which was just as well. The truth of what had happened to me was too overwhelming for her to handle.

When they found out I would move to Germany, they suggested I leave from D.C., so they could see me off as I left the country. Reluctantly, I agreed.

My last month in the States would be at the end of April and in early May. I packed my few belongings and headed from the Smith home to Marietta. There, I reconnected with Jessica and spent time with her two boys, Steve and Brandon, whom I used to babysit. Jessica was no longer serving food at Torch and Candle, but was still serving to an exclusive clientele at various high-end restaurants. She and Mort had divorced, and she was living with Johnny Cantrell. Indeed, one of those strapping Cantrell brothers. Brandon, three, and Steve, nine, were older now, but I still considered them my own. It was so good to spend time with friends, and as much as I hated to leave them, I knew living in Germany would be exciting. Anywhere in Europe would be great. It would be reminiscent of Argentina, and I was ready.

I missed my mom, but I had no genuine desire to see my father as I still felt some animosity toward him. Although I dreaded fielding any topic related to my life for the past two years, I was more hurt that they never inquired beyond a perfunctory "How are you?" We mostly sat in silence in their Marietta motel room, the first time I had seen them in two years. That they had abandoned me in midtown Atlanta never came up. We never discussed the harrowing events that became my life. That they moved to another city within weeks of dumping me was never explained. It was as if a contentious day had never transpired between us. Typical of the Flynn style, it was all about appearances.

The lame show *Hee Haw* was droning on the TV in the background, offering great relief. At one point, when my father had gone into the bathroom, my mother leaned over to me and whispered, "I think daddy will be putting you back in his will now." I had never even contemplated a will. So, not only had he abandoned me, but then taken me out of his will, to boot? *What an ass.*

At 17 years old, I was still mired in confusion about what had unfolded in my life during the past two years, the past four years honestly. Ever since moving back to the States, life had a surreal quality. I had accumulated a mountain of self-disgust, along with a healthy dose of disdain toward my father, even if I couldn't articulate why. *Was I the cheap, loose girl my father had come to view me as?* Occasionally, I would give myself kudos for having survived the shit I had encountered along the way.

Daddy arrived at Jessica's apartment and loaded my suitcase into his newest baby, a blue Buick Skylark. As with all of his cars, it was in mint condition, polished, shiny, and immaculate inside and out. After some difficult goodbyes to Jessica and the boys, I rode off with my parents and we headed north to Washington D.C.

During the trip, my father got a speeding ticket. "Well, that just ruined a lifetime record. I wouldn't have been speeding if not for Stephanie saying she was hungry," he complained, unsolicited. Neither mother nor I responded, both grateful that he at least didn't blame my mom. I could accept the assigned guilt for her now that I no longer had to live with him.

Daddy's over-the-top table manners were on full display, with one major change. He picked up his sandwich with his hands to eat it. This seemingly inconsequential act intrigued me, and I wondered if it signaled liberation in other areas as well. I decided to forgo the potato chips that came with my tuna on wheat sandwich. Not because I didn't want to upset Daddy, but rather, I didn't want to disappoint Martin. I wanted to maintain the healthy lifestyle that Martin had imbued in me.

I reflected on the past two years as we traversed the miles along I-85 north. Despite my age, I had grown into adulthood in most regards, no doubt. I was much more emotionally stable now, as well. The rape, abortion, living with Lionel, having to sell myself — all taught me about the precariousness of life, the dangers, the pain, the unknowns, and the need to adapt to your immediate circumstances — but most of all, resilience. And on the other side, the grace of life, the gifts from strangers, the love of friends. Gratitude. Hope. An unwavering belief that with resilience and hope, one could conquer whatever life threw their way.

I hoped and prayed that one day no girl or woman would ever have to go through another deadly illegal abortion. I hoped that one day, medical professionals would perform abortions in a safe environment with someone close by to provide emotional support.

Further into our drive to D.C., a box truck ahead of us, driving in the left lane, blew a tire. We watched in horror as the box full of bread and pastries swayed back and forth, on the verge of tipping over. The driver waved his left arm out of his window, using only his right arm to steer the behemoth back into control. Miraculously, he straightened the truck and came to a full stop on the left shoulder. My father had quickly maneuvered into the left lane, blocking other traffic from approaching the truck, and to my surprise, he pulled onto the shoulder behind it. He turned on the emergency flashers and got out of the car to talk to the driver. After a long discussion, he returned to the car. "Ted is his name. I commended him for handling that box truck so well. His left arm is handicapped, so that recovery was even more challenging and remarkable. I got his boss' name and phone number and plan to let him know how well this employee of his performed in such a precarious situation. He should be applauded for how well he handled himself and the company property," he concluded. That was the father I had looked up to as a child, the one who cared about others enough to stop and help. More bits of hope.

That night, we arrived in D.C. late and took a quick tour of their luxury apartment on the 15th floor of the elegant River House complex. The plush yellow carpet throughout their apartment was inviting and unique for the era, as were the warm blue sofa and coordinating chairs nearby. I could still see my parents' love for antiques, and I recognized all the pieces that they had shipped up from Argentina, most of which they had stored while we were living in the little apartment in Atlanta. These rooms were much larger and accommodated their ample collection with the stately elegance they commanded. After such a long drive and the brief tour, we were tired and went to bed.

I was glad to hear golf on the TV when I woke up that Saturday morning. Daddy didn't sanction talking while his golf was on, which meant mother and I would have to be quiet and there was no pressure to keep up a conversation. Mother spent the day bustling in the kitchen, as she always used to. I went through my clothes and rearranged them since I had mostly thrown them into the suitcase while packing. While out circling their complex, I stopped by the massive outdoor pool. I took a break on one of the lounge chairs and yearned for a cigarette.

That night at dinner, I enjoyed eating one of my mom's home-cooked meals after two years without one. She made my favorite — pork chops, rice, peas, and applesauce. I recognized her thoughtfulness and thanked her. I didn't eat the pork chops, explaining that I was now a vegetarian, eating only tuna occasionally. They seemed to be cool with it.

I attempted to bring some humor to our dinner conversation and brought up our old Arlington neighbors, the Flanagans. "Whenever I think of D.C., I can't help but be reminded of the Flanagans. Tina, Kathy, and Mrs. Trudy Flanagan were great neighbors. They were a fun family."

"Oh, my," Mother began, "what a family they were, indeed. Do you remember the story about little Tina taking her mom Trudy's big black bra to Kindergarten for Show and Tell?" We all laughed, even Daddy.

"And then, after all the lectures from her parents and privileges taken away, she did it again three weeks later, taking her black girdle!"

Departing for West Germany the following morning felt eerily similar to the morning my father woke me and ordered me to pack my belongings and be ready to leave in 30 minutes. This time, I understood the tears in Mother's eyes while she stood at the front door. "I love you, Stephanie," she said warmly.

"I love you, Mom. Bye." We both knew it would be years before we would see each other again. Bittersweet, and yet necessary.

Daddy drove me to Dulles International Airport, and we

rode mostly in silence. When we arrived at Dulles, he pulled up at the drop-off zone and put the car in park. He got out, retrieved my suitcase from the back, and walked me just inside the airport doors. He put my suitcase down and, with a quick hug and goodbye, went back to his Buick. That was it. We were done. Again. This time, it would be for good. He was no longer accountable for my wellbeing, no longer responsible for me legally.

I couldn't wait to get on the airplane. Filled with newfound hope, I was on my way to a resurrected life reminiscent of the years in my beloved Argentina. I would start anew, a fledgling adult, an Army wife in beautiful and delightful Ansbach, West Germany.

∼

Conclusion — Part One

PHOTOS

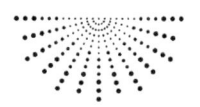

My Mother, a pilot in the WASP during World War II, with her airplane

Castle Front

Castle Back

Family Portrait - Attaché House, Buenos Aires, Argentina

Daddy, Steppa, Melissa and Ivette First Communion

Steppa with Gordy, Jr. and their Shepherds Lobo and Gina

My Nanny, Emma, with our German Shepherds Lobo and Gina

VESTIGES OF LIGHT

My mother's favorite picture of me as a toddler

Stephanie, 8th grade school picture

Stephanie, just turned 16, Gay, Georgia

Me with baby Abi, 18 years old in Ansbach

PART II
THE CHARMER'S WIFE

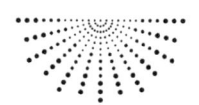

"Your legacy is every life you touch" - Maya Angelou

32
ANSBACH, WEST GERMANY

"I am going to make everything around me beautiful ... that will be my life" - Elise de Wolfe

Martin found us a quaint apartment about two miles from the busy army base in Ansbach, a small city about 25 miles southwest of Nuremberg, Germany. Our little apartment landed on the third and top floor of a six-unit building. In our shared building, we found comfort among fellow Americans. A tiny kitchen with a small dining table, a living space, and a bedroom were all part of our unit. Our one bath with a shower was off of the kitchen. With no air conditioning, we were often hot during the summer months. Fall and winter, we had an oil heater to keep the place warm.

Martin reported to a base further out of town and

commuted there each day on his moped. He bought me a 10-speed bike as my mode of transportation, and I quickly adapted to being a bike rider. It was easy in Europe — their streets and sidewalks all accommodated bicycles. I carried a backpack with me all the time in case I stopped to get food on the way home from wherever I had gone. The backpack also carried groceries from the base exchange and laundry back and forth from home. I became physically strong during those years.

Living in a European country was heaven to me. It felt like Argentina. It felt like home. I didn't care much for the German language, though, and only learned enough of it to get myself around town for shopping and necessities. The bustling farmers' market, aromatic bakeries, and cheese shops were among my favorite haunts. Nothing quite compared to the simple pleasure of sinking my teeth into a warm bröchen roll hosting some pungent cheese and a dollop of luscious fruit jam.

Our local Brewhaus, conveniently located down Schiller Strasse from our building, served as Martin's sanctuary after a long day's work, where he would pick up his nightly assortment of beers. Initially, it took about four beers for him to escape the confines of his restless mind and plunge into a vegetative state, seeking solace in an alternate reality devoid of human connection. Regrettably, this alternate reality soon became a regular fixture, demanding half a dozen to a dozen beers, coupled with shots of schnapps, whiskey, or bourbon. Witnessing the transformation into a mere shell of his former self left me bewildered, saddened, and often enraged. I was ill-equipped to comprehend the complexities of addiction and its connected struggles. My days were spent vigilantly monitoring his every move, desperately attempting to prevent any stupid behavior. Yet, my efforts were not always successful, as he would occasionally resort to peeing out of our third-story window or attempting to venture outside clad only in his underwear. A constant battle ensued, exacerbated by his ill-fated decision to relieve himself in our oil heater, extinguishing the very flames that provided us warmth. With determination, I would haul a cumbersome canister down into the basement, fill it to the brim with fuel, then trudge up three flights of stairs to feed our oil heater and keep it running.

The Army facilitated cigarette smoking and alcohol consumption, making them highly accessible and affordable. Across small towns in Europe, young, intoxicated, and lustful U.S. servicemen infiltrated the scene. Amidst this atmosphere, Martin cleverly earned extra income by selling American cigarettes and alcohol to fellow Germans. Not only was it profitable, but he earned respect from the locals, with restaurants occasionally treating us to free meals.

33
THE BIG NEWS

"I'm not telling you it is going to be easy. I'm telling you it's going to be worth it." - Art Williams

Life was quickly becoming more difficult, as I came to realize Martin had a serious drinking problem. Then, in the fall of 1973, at 17 years old, I found myself pregnant. I broke the news to Martin, now 24, as we were out eating pizza at one of our favorite spots around the corner from home. He was not pleased. "How'd this happen?" he asked. I knew fatherhood was not something he'd ever mentioned aspiring to. If he didn't even want to be married, he likely wouldn't want the traditional kids that came with that ritual, either. Not to mention his constant dread of supporting anyone besides himself.

"Remember when you were in Grafenwöhr for three weeks, of training?" I reminded him. "When Bonnie and I came for a visit that long weekend, I forgot my birth control pills, but you said it wouldn't matter, I would probably not get pregnant just missing them for a couple of days. You also said you'd pull out. So much for that working."

"Well, the army will pay for an abortion. They don't offer them here at our base, but you can go to England and get one there. They will pay your entire way," he tried to encourage me. "How far along are you, do you know?"

"I'm not sure," I answered. "The first pregnancy test showed a false negative, so there's really no telling until I see a doctor. I really don't want to go through another abortion. It's a risk I don't really want to take. Besides, the army will pay for having a baby."

Irritated that I wouldn't consent to getting another abortion, he followed up with, "I hope you're prepared to pay for all this baby's gear, 'cause I won't be contributing to it. You'll have to cover it all with what's left of your $145 monthly allotment check." *There it was. I knew that was coming.* It hurt me deeply. He couldn't fathom wanting or loving a child of his own.

"That's fine," I snapped back, pissed. *What an ass,* I thought. *He's worried about the financial burden, and he wants nothing to do with the baby.* "I can still be a wonderful mother," I said, my voice filled with confidence, beyond my youth. "I've always loved children so much, and I'm sure I can do a good job at this, no matter how young I am. I can handle this. It's not worth the risk of getting another abortion."

As it was, I was already paying a percentage of all our combined bills for rent, utilities, and food. The amount was based on my percentage of income against Martin's. That was the percentage amount I was required to pay for each bill. I had learned to be really savvy with my money. I knew it was so limited, and yet I figured out I could manage buying the baby's needs as long as I bought all used stuff. That would prove easy, as, like cigarettes and booze, the army life trapped most couples into becoming parents as well. Babies were free if you didn't request a TV in your post-birth room. If you did, it was a $10 charge for three days. The local army newspaper, The Stars and Stripes, had a slew of ads for cribs, clothes, diapers, bottles, toys, and every kind of baby gear. As families returned to the U.S., they unloaded all of their belongings. Only officers made enough money to afford to ship their households home. Most of us left with our clothes and not much else.

That night, while lying there restless in bed, I thought back to my two abortions. The first one left a profound wound that I knew would be a part of me forever. The second one was unexpected, and the surrounding circumstances were strange. It was not long after my recovery from the first one that I missed a period. Martin took me to the free clinic behind the Crisis Center to get a pregnancy test. It came back positive, and we were distraught. It just couldn't be happening again. We languished. The clinic would cover the abortion cost, presumably through Planned Parenthood. Because abortions were actually legal in New York, the clinic expected you to pay your own airfare, and they would cover the rest of the expenses. We had no money for a plane ticket, so Martin resorted to calling his parents for the funds to cover my flight to New York, explaining about the unintended pregnancy. Reluctantly, they purchased the round-trip ticket for us.

On the flight to New York, all of us in the front half of the economy section were going for abortions. I sat next to an older woman wearing a neutral business suit with an elegant white shirt. Her perfectly coiffed hair helped exude a "professional mom" feeling, and she mentioned she was too old to start over with a baby and was therefore traveling to New York for this abortion. I didn't offer her any details of my need for one, but nodded along, agreeing with her. I still harbored a distrust of adults and avoided disclosing anything to them when possible.

We arrived at La Guardia Airport, and the airport staff shuffled us off the airplane onto a bus. The bus driver steered us through the downtown areas, and I absorbed everything I could from the large windows. It reminded me of downtown Buenos Aires — all the tall buildings, taxis, cars, buses, and concrete, with a spattering of trees now and then. The people were all walking quickly, their heads down, driving against the fall winds. I felt the awe of the city and only wished my first visit there could have been under other circumstances. Less ominous ones.

After the procedure, I woke up in a cot-like bed in a large room filled with portable beds and other women. Most of them were dressed, eating cookies, and looked ready to leave. The anesthesia was working overtime, and the nurses kept trying to wake me up. I was really out of it.

A doctor in a white lab coat came and sat on the side of my cot before I could get up to find those cookies I desperately wanted. He started off, "Stephanie, you weren't pregnant. We're not sure if there was an error in the pregnancy test you took, or what went wrong here, but you didn't need an abortion." I was shocked.

Here I was a year later, pondering the events of that frosty day in New York City. I wondered if that doctor recognized my young age and chose to spare me the emotional grief of an abortion.

34
THE HOLIDAYS OVERSEAS

"The exhaustion of this reality ..." - Joy Reid

Oktoberfest came along, and Martin was giddy with anticipation. He and his friends had partied and celebrated the year before and loved it all. We went with some friends and other GIs and took part in the local brew fest, held in a large tent that was crowded with GIs and Germans. The hefty German servers were the strongest women I'd ever seen. They could carry at least four, if not six, beer steins in each hand, foam sloshing around and out, and everyone soaking up the airborne spills like kids capturing snowflakes in the air.

On our walk home, we stopped at a friend's apartment to drop them off. Martin was completely wasted and could barely stay upright. As we stood outside saying our goodbyes by their white picket fence, Martin swayed backwards, ready to fall into the fence. I stretched my arm around his back to stop him, and he turned around and shoved me into the fence, my back getting stabbed with one of the pickets. Without a second thought, I punched his face and hit his left temple. He was furious and started screaming at me, and I yelled back, "I'm not going to get shoved around by you. I was trying to help you! Fuck you!" We headed toward home, each of us walking on opposite sides of the now empty five-lane road, yelling at each other across the avenue all the way back.

"I'm sending you back to the States, dammit. I don't want you or a baby," he hollered across the roadway. That stung. Tears streamed down my face as I panicked at the thought of having to support myself and a baby alone. I resolved that night that I would not spend my life with an alcoholic. Whether he sent me home to the U.S. or not, I would start planning my exit from this sham of a marriage. Martin gradually released his anger toward me, conveniently ignoring the fact that he instigated the altercation by pushing me backward. I was unsure whether he forgave me or if he forgot about it completely in his constant state of blackout drunkenness. I wasn't dissuaded from starting an escape plan.

Our first Thanksgiving, we invited a group of Martin's GI friends over to eat with us. I had never cooked a turkey but got a recipe sent through the mail from Mother. I still have the used scrap of paper where she wrote out the instructions step-by-step that involved putting the whole turkey and pan in a paper bag and sealing it up. It sounded absurd, but to my surprise, the turkey was flawless. I still roast turkeys in a paper-bag-covered pan. We borrowed a table to put in front of the sofa bed, placed all the available chairs on the opposite side, and crammed in the eight of us to share our feast. The spread included Martin's family cheese squash recipe, along with classic sides like mashed potatoes, peas, stuffing cooked inside the turkey, and a can of cranberry sauce. Everyone loved it. It felt great to spend the holiday with the guys, creating memories together.

That Christmas brought a letter from my older brother, Gordy, admonishing me never to upset our mother again. "Don't ever cause our mother pain in your lifetime again. She is a kind, sweet woman, and an exceptional mother. She doesn't deserve any more hurt from you," he wrote. I read between the lines of his admonishing letter and gathered that he was on board with my parents' choice to abandon me at the Crisis Center. I looked up to my big brother all of my life, but now he was not holding back. Disappointing him was unbearable. Overwhelmed by sadness, I cried helplessly. I vowed never to hurt my mother or disappoint my brother Gordy again. I didn't answer his letter. Rather, I lived out my response with devotion to our mother. I made sure that all our communications made her laugh.

Martin and I spent our first New Year's in Germany apart, and I missed the opportunity to celebrate together. Martin took a trip to Amsterdam with his buddy, Booker, and didn't invite me to go with them. I joined the neighbors in our building outside for a small celebration. I was three months pregnant and drank nothing. At midnight, they all turned to kiss their spouses, and I had no one, leaving me feeling dejected and alone. Martin returned and zealously described Amsterdam's infamous red-light district, where women casually displayed themselves nude in windows, and the unmistakable scent of marijuana filled the air. They had a blast.

Martin's drinking was so problematic at this point that it was not uncommon for his buddies to bring him home with his arms draped around their necks as his feet barely dragged the ground. He collapsed onto our bed and snored the night away. I cried myself to sleep and questioned why it had to be this way. Martin was incredibly intelligent and could excel at anything he wanted to, but instead he was a falling-down drunk at 24 years old.

35
PREPPING FOR OUR BABY

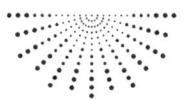

"A baby fills a place in your heart that you never knew was empty." - Unknown

I managed to purchase all the necessities for a newborn and found myself as organized and ready as I could be for our baby to be born. The only thing left for me to do was get my GED. I didn't want to be a teen mother who didn't have a high school diploma. At the base, I got the test instructions and was told about prep classes they would offer in the coming weeks. That was something I didn't have time for. I went in and took the test, cold turkey. I passed it. Check.

I found a crib, baby clothes, stroller, a Johnny-Jump-Up, and a baby carrier, from the base's newspaper ads. The rest of my necessities came through the PX on base. I splurged and bought a few new rattles and unisex pajamas since we didn't know what gender our baby would be. I was so pleased with all my preparedness for this big life change.

There he was. In a store window, looking out at me beseechingly. He was the cutest stuffed monkey I had ever seen, three feet tall and made of a fuzzy patchwork fabric. It was instant love. He was expensive, so I asked Martin to share the cost. It meant so much to me to get this stuffed animal. He said he would think about it. Then, one day soon after, while we were walking home, we passed the children's park near our home. Martin stopped and told me that if I could go down the monkey bars and back, he would pay for half of the stuffed monkey I wanted so badly. I knew this was my only chance, and I had to take it. My enormous belly waddled down one side of the bars and then struggled up the other, but I made it. The following week, we bought the monkey. I was so proud of myself, knowing the feat I accomplished was worthy of praise, considering how pregnant I was.

Our precious baby girl was born the first week of June 1974, just as expected. At our base we had three doctors who took care of the pregnant women: a dermatologist, a vet, and a brain surgeon. The brain surgeon was the roughest, the dermatologist was a nerd, and the vet, our favorite. He had a bedside manner of respect, gentleness, and dignity.

The dermatologist was on duty when I walked from home to the base at 7:30 am, in labor. We had to stop every few minutes to let a contraction come. It was daunting, but I knew we had to get to the base to catch an ambulance to Nuremberg, where we delivered our babies. Dr. Derm didn't think I was far along enough to leave yet, so he sent me to walk around the base. I didn't make it 20 feet before I almost collapsed from a painful contraction. Martin ran to tell him as I trudged up the stairs again. Dr. Derm checked me again and called for Irene, the Scottish nurse, to ride in the ambulance with us the 30 miles to the Nuremberg Army base. We had a young Hispanic driver, "Chicano," was how Martin described him. We weren't out of Ansbach before I felt the need to push. Irene put her hand inside my vagina and told the driver to rush. He threw the lights and sirens on, and we flew down the road. Lying on the stretcher, I could see poles and trees flashing by. Martin was sweating profusely, as was the driver. If we didn't make it to Nuremberg, the driver and Irene would have to deliver the baby themselves on the side of the road. We made it to Nuremberg in record time. They pulled me onto the operating table in the OR, straight from the gurney, avoiding the dreaded enema. As I moaned, the nurse by my side admonished curtly and loudly, "We don't need any sound effects." I lay still and in utter silence. They quickly delivered my beautiful baby girl with thick, dark hair and a graceful face, precious Abi.

I loved having a baby to love and to love me back. We would never abandon each other. We were bonded for life. Abigail cried a lot and pulled her legs up close to her chest, seemingly in stomach pain. I tried feeding her, but that made it worse, and she spit up a lot. I held her close, and that is where she found peace and sleep. The Snuggli pack I had saved up for and purchased through the Whole Earth Catalog rescued me. I carried Abigail around in it so she could be close, warm, and secure, and we spent the first six months of her life tethered like this, needing and helping each other. I knew the odds were against me as a teenage mother. We were the questionable girls, the high school dropouts, the dregs of society. I was determined to prove them all wrong, dammit. I refused to be just a good teen mom. My sole goal was to be a wonderful mother. Period. Motherhood became my life's focus. I would show my parents how to do it better. I would show society at large how to do it better, and nothing would stop me. Raising children became my focus, and I learned everything I could about it. From growth, to behavior, to nutrition, to psychology, I covered all my bases. It was hard to find suitable reading materials, but I devoured anything and everything I could get my hands on related to rearing children. My Dr. Spock and Adelle Davis books became worn out, dog-eared, and yellowed.

Martin was completely enchanted with our baby girl, and I thought for a bit that he might actually come around, drink less and become more normal now that he was a father. He quickly returned to drinking until he blacked out. I now had two people to take care of — the drunk and the baby. Abigail and I often cried together until we drifted off to sleep. I resented Martin. I felt scared and insecure all the time because of his alcoholism. Although I felt guilty for always crying, it was the only way I knew to relieve the pent-up angst and tension.

I resolved I would not have my daughter living in a home with a falling-down drunk for a father. As soon as I returned to the States, I would waste no time leaving him. I opened a savings account in my name only and continued to squirrel away money from my monthly allotment check. Ten dollars here and $20 there, I accumulated funds for my escape, and it felt good to have a plan set into motion.

36
RETURN TO THE U.S.A

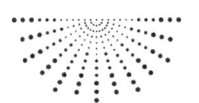

"Sometimes you have to accept the fact that certain things will never go back to how they used to be." - Unknown

Martin's father had a heart attack in November 1974, at home, in Gay, Georgia. His mother, Phil, a nurse, and brother, Aaron, gave him mouth-to-mouth resuscitation and chest compressions, trying to revive him, to no avail. He died in the ambulance on his way to an Atlanta hospital.

Since Martin was due to finish his two years in the army by December, they offered him an early leave. He said he would wait to make sure he got all of his benefits rather than use them up. He was not close to his father and didn't mind missing his funeral. I, on the other hand, loved Martin, Sr. He was so good to me when I lived there with them. The way he loved and cared for me made me feel like his own daughter. It was refreshing, delightful yet strange, comforting yet unsettling and unfamiliar to me. I loved his mom, too, but his dad held a really special place in my heart.

While living on the apple farm in Gay, Georgia, with the Smith family, my world expanded, and I loved every minute there with them. Although I missed Martin terribly and couldn't wait until I could go to Germany to be with him.

Living on an apple farm meant we had the fruit available to us most any time. One day, I baked the family a 'healthy' version of apple pie that I had learned to make. In the crust, you used whole wheat flour instead of white flour. Of course, you had to add sugar to make it palatable. I was so proud of my perfectly golden topped pie and couldn't wait for everyone to try it. Aaron was the first to gag and leave the room, pie plate in hand. I didn't think too much of it until Martin Sr. went to the kitchen and Phil struggled and came out with, "Is there supposed to be sugar in the crust?" I took my own bite to discover I had completely forgotten to put the sugar in the crust mix. It was horrible. Repulsive. Not edible, to say the least. I put my plate down in the kitchen and went upstairs to my room and crawled under the bedcovers, in tears. It was so humiliating. I had failed. I knew how to make that pie. How could I have forgotten the sugar? Within a few minutes, Martin Sr. came into my room and sat on the side of my bed. He started telling me stories about Phil's cooking misadventures in her younger years. The time she forgot to turn the oven on to cook the Thanksgiving turkey, and they didn't realize it for hours. The time she forgot about the soup, she let it boil dry and scorch the pot. There were several of these cooking mishaps and he had me giggling and then laughing in no time. That night, he taught me the value of self-deprecating humor. It was a well-learned lesson, demonstrated to me with compassion, caring, and a wink. I loved him so much. I was pretty devastated that he was now gone. He would never get to meet his treasured first grandchild, Abigail.

After Martin's two-year stint was up at the beginning of 1975, we moved back to the U.S. I had a 12-hour flight ahead of me, with 7-month-old Abigail, who was finally showing signs of feeling better. Although I made all of her baby food by hand, from scratch, I relented and bought some jarred Gerber baby food for the long airplane ride home. It would just work more easily all around. I flew home prepared with the Snuggli baby pack, plenty of diapers, and jarred baby food. Our formidable flight went beautifully. Abi cried only briefly to let me know she was hungry. I was so relieved upon touching down at Dulles that she had been so good. A woman seated diagonally behind me leaned forward and said in her German accent, "You are an excellent mother," with a warm smile on her face. That comment meant the world to me. I glowed as I meekly thanked her. I was so proud of myself for those few moments. It felt surreal. I felt validated.

My parents, especially my father, were thrilled to meet baby Abigail, and he was smitten. It was as if she were his. While I was nursing her and covered up with a blanket, he walked over, uncovered me, and stared at us. I felt completely repulsed and terribly uncomfortable. It lasted only a few moments but felt like an eternity.

I was in D.C. for only two days, mercifully. My feelings about my parents were very conflicted. I gained a new outlook from becoming a parent. The thought of ever abandoning my Abi seemed out of the question.

I then flew to Atlanta, where Jessica picked me up at the

airport. In my excitement to see her, I forgot about Abigail being on my back in the Snuggli, and knocked her head into the car door frame as I was getting into it. She howled and cried, but only briefly. I felt horrible and so irresponsible. *Shit! How do you forget about carrying your baby on your back?*

Jessica and the boys were my soul family and my saviors. They were my connection to normalcy, whatever that looked like in my life. Steve, now 12, became Abigail's first babysitter. I had not left her side since she was born, and it was time to let a sitter take care of her, at least briefly. I had not allowed myself a break from baby Abi for over seven months. My youth carried me well, but the emotional strain was considerable. Abi grew past the phase of an irritable stomach and was eating, and sleeping normally, finally. I went grocery shopping one afternoon while Steve cared for her. Having some of the pressure of new motherhood lifted, I felt exhilarated, and I returned from my shopping to find a sleeping baby and Steve watching television near her.

37
MOVING TO MARIETTA, GA

"The only way to make sense out of change is to plunge into it, move with it, and join the dance." - Alan Watts

Martin and I got an apartment in the same complex where Jessica and Johnny Cantrell now lived in Marietta, next to I-75, heading into Atlanta. Johnny, another one of the handsome Cantrell boys, was Ted's brother and a friend from Ridgeview High days. He was the head maintenance man at the complex and, as part of his compensation for work, lived in a free apartment. Jessica waited tables, and their lives seemed stable.

Martin volunteered at the farmer's market co-op downtown for food. He received a nice chunk of money when he left the army, so we managed rent with his payout. I started looking for a job and found one working at a nearby day care center. I had the toddler room and loved being with the children. My GED and lack of college limited the work I could find.

There was one pretty rowdy boy that no other teachers liked — Sammy. I gave Sam my attention and care and could get through to him. He listened to me because he liked and respected me, and I, him. I talked to his father and found out he had no mother, just his dad. It was a daily struggle for his father, and he appreciated me so much for taking the time to nurture Sammy.

Three months after returning to the States, in March 1975, I let Martin know I planned to leave the marriage. He cared little, and to forget about the breakup of our family, he went off to get drunk and high. Consistently in a state of drunkenness, he had no specific direction, aim, or goals. He tried to justify delivering newspapers as a full-time job. "You get up early to start your day, the birds are waking, and the stillness is beautiful." I didn't care if he wanted to deliver papers or shovel shit, as long as he was out of my life. His alcoholism became unbearable, and all I wanted was to escape from him. I developed a strong aversion towards booze and its negative impact and much preferred the buzz from smoking pot instead, seeming safer and nonviolent.

On June 1st, Abigail and I moved into our own little rental house on St. John Avenue in Marietta, Georgia, north of Atlanta. I was terrified to forge ahead on my own with only a day-care job to rely on and wasn't sure how I would make it financially. I had to take a little pocket calculator to the grocery store with me to make sure I only bought what I could afford. My father sent me $50 a month and sometimes, up to $100. Rent was $250, and these stipends helped quite a bit. I was grateful but also puzzled by his willingness to help me. I still carried the full weight of being declared "an incorrigible teenager" and wasn't sure why Daddy would help now. For every check received, I sent him a handwritten thank-you note.

It wasn't long before I quit my minimum wage day care job and started caring for children in my home in order to make enough money to survive. Sammy came with me, as did little Ellen from daycare, and Jessica's son, Brandon. It allowed me to make some more money and also, most importantly, be home with Abigail. The kids loved her so much and doted on her every move. She thrived in our new environment, and I felt some relief and joy for the first time in a long while. Always the optimist, I managed to look past the scary parts and envision a fruitful life ahead for us. These daydreams sustained me, often.

38
JOHN O'BRIEN

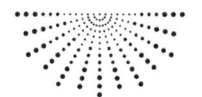

"New love can heal lost loves, but it cannot make you forget."
- Jennifer Megan Varnadore

In March 1975, I met Johnny's maintenance helper, John O'Brien. He was well built and handsome. His hair was on the longish side, blonde and wavy, matching well with his striking big blue eyes and soft facial features. The Chattahoochee River Race in Atlanta was our first group activity together. We were doomed from the beginning, as our inflatable raft blew out on one side. As luck would have it, though, another couple had the same problem with their raft on the opposite side. We tied our rafts together and off we went, floating down the mighty river. People packed the water, with beer and bikinis abounding. Halfway through the race, our raft started taking on water pretty badly. O'Brien took off his outer flannel shirt and wrapped it around me, trying to warm up my shivers. I saw him as a gentleman, and that really caught my attention. I didn't feel guilty at all for liking him or spending time with him, as Martin had left our marriage long before and I had already announced my intentions to leave him.

Martin spent all of his time downtown with his own group of friends. He had essentially moved all his personal belongings out of the apartment and to somewhere downtown, but I didn't know where. He was waiting until I found a place of my own to divide up the rest of our meager possessions. A pull-down desk, a little 13-inch black-and-white TV, a fairly nice stereo and a double bed mattress were all that we owned. He took the desk and stereo, and I took the TV and bed mattress. With no money to pay for a divorce, separating would have to do for now.

John O'Brien and I started spending a lot of time together and became an item. He took me on dirt bike rides in the woods, on his Enduro motorcycle, which I loved. By the time I moved into my little place on St. John Avenue, it was John who helped me move in. I didn't care that I was jumping from one relationship to another. I was just grateful that someone would want me. As a teenager with a one-year-old child, I wasn't exactly life-partner material for a great guy. That John O'Brien even wanted a relationship with me had me praising the gratitude gods. I was so afraid of being alone, and now I wouldn't be. He cherished little Abi and assumed a father-figure role seamlessly. I thought I'd hit the lottery.

Life was tough, but at least it wasn't as tough as living with a drunk. I worried Martin would drive drunk with Abi in the car or get drunk and not take care of her whenever he came to pick her up. I had no choice, though. As her father, he had visitation rights. When Abi was with her father, I sometimes drank cheap wine to numb my mind temporarily and escape the worrying. I wasn't concerned about becoming an alcoholic, because the only time I over-imbibed, I had to be carried out of the bar by Johnny Cantrell and one of his friends and was sick as a dog. That level of humiliation was enough to stop me from overindulging again.

As John and I got more serious in our relationship, I felt the need to tell him all about my past. I believed any man considering a partnership with me deserved to know about my buried secrets. He didn't seem to care much, and the history he shared with me seemed so tame in comparison. His last serious relationship was with a girl in California who had a young son of Mexican-American descent. She broke off their engagement, but he never clarified why except to give me the proverbial, "she wanted to stay single and independent."

About six weeks into our relationship, John drove me up to the corner dirt biking hill to park and talk. He said he wanted us to be exclusive with each other, and I happily agreed. I belonged. I was someone's girlfriend. It felt good. It helped me feel safe. I couldn't wait to tell Jessica and Johnny that John and I were officially a couple now. I knew they'd be happy for me.

John shared an apartment with his best friend, Freddie. Together with their mutual friend, Greg, and of course Johnny, they made a hilarious foursome. They were funny, good-looking, strong, musical, dirt bike enthusiasts, and all-around good guys with cool girlfriends and wives. As we spent more time together as a group, we became close friends. They were my family. It felt so wonderful, and I was so grateful. Abi was lovingly and wholeheartedly accepted by them as one of their own. There was nothing quite like camping together in the North Georgia mountains, hammocks under the stars, fires burning, food grilling, beer flowing, pot smoking, swims in the river, and endless conversations.

I was so grateful for these friends of John's the night I broke down on I-75/85 North, going from Atlanta up to Marietta. Of course it was in the Saab. My dash lights were all out, so at 10:30 pm I couldn't see anything at all on the dashboard. I noticed a little red light was on, but I did not know what it meant. I soon found out as the Saab lost all power and I had to drift off to the right shoulder to bring it to a full stop.

Panic quickly set in. On the backseat floorboard, I had a pound of pot. I bought the pound for $250 and expected to sell it, generating a $400 return, resulting in a $150 profit. It was more than half of my $250 rent. I needed the extra income for bills and car repairs, obviously. I knew it was a risky move, but I thought for sure it would all work out seamlessly. *Fuck. What now? How would I get my ass home and then back here to get the pot out of the car?* Especially before any cops could come by and shine a flashlight into the car and see my weed-filled knapsack. If they had any suspicions, they could just force their way into the car.

I realized I needed to flag down a passing car to get a ride home. I found a white paper napkin that I promptly started waving out my open car window, trying not to show the shaking in my scared hands. It only took one or two cars passing by before an 18-wheeler swung onto the right shoulder and screeched its brakes, bringing the rig to a stop. After backing up his rig slowly, he jumped out quickly, and I saw him flash a wide smile, revealing a gap where his two front teeth should have been. He looked like an overweight ex-football player. His black hair waved behind him and rested on his shoulders. I could almost *feel* the hair on his arms; it was so profuse. The toothless brute walked briskly toward my car and, as my headlights shone on him, I grew more terrified with each step he took.

"What's goin' on dear," he started out in his deep, resounding voice. I wasn't sure what to expect, and all my feelers were up and waving madly.

"I'm not sure," I answered right away, nervously. "The car has had a lot of problems but this time there was no warning. It just quit."

"You probably ran out of gas, hon," he continued booming over to me in his thick southern accent.

"Well, my dashboard lights don't work, so I can't see the gas gauge," I lamented. It was always some damn thing with cars in my world. Before he could say anything else, I interjected, "My husband is going to be so worried about where I am so late! He expected me back 30 minutes ago. I wonder if he has called the police looking for me yet." I wanted this guy to think people were waiting for me, even though no one was.

"Well, my name is Ron, and I would be glad to drive you home in my rig, if you want," he offered. I knew I was taking a colossal risk getting into a stranger's truck, but I weighed my options and took a reading of my gut and went with him. Providing him with my St. John Avenue address, he drove me straight to my front door. I couldn't understand how he maneuvered his 18-wheeler through those narrow neighborhood streets, but in my desperate and fearful situation, he proved to be a very kind and helpful gentleman. His selfless gesture was appreciated beyond measure.

Now I faced the angst of the pot left in the car on the Interstate. I called John right away and actually woke him up as I bellowed into the phone what all had happened. He and Freddy got up and went down to retrieve the Saab and the pound of pot. The entire episode dissuaded me from continuing any weed dealings. I realized it was just too risky.

39
THE BLONDE

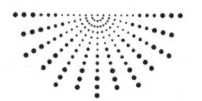

"There's a reason why two people stay together - they give each other something they think nobody else can."
- Unknown

It was a given that John and I spent weekend nights together, and on one particular Friday night, he hadn't called yet to make any plans. I tried calling him repeatedly, but all I got was a busy signal. I surmised the phone had been knocked off the base and John probably didn't even know it. He was likely wondering why he hadn't heard from me as well. I got into my car and drove over to his apartment in the old four-plex he lived in on busy Powder Springs Road. It looked like the power was out. No lights were on, and it was really quiet, except for a woman's voice coming from Freddy's room; the bed area. I walked up the couple of steps and knocked on the screen door that led into the apartment via Freddy's room. The only response I received was a clear "uh-oh," from a voice I recognized as Freddy's. Right away, I sensed things wouldn't be good.

Letting myself in, I could see Freddy lying propped up on his bed, naked under the sheets, with a strange chick beside him whom I'd never seen before. I immediately walked into John's dark room, and there he was — with her. The long-haired blonde bimbo spouted, "Hi! How are you?" with the feigned innocence of a young child. I felt numb, trying to keep my weak knees from buckling. Devastation. My world was crumbling beneath me with no way to save myself. We would end before even really getting started. I would immediately be back in complete vulnerability with no one to have my back, so to speak. Living on my own was unaffordable. I wanted to be swallowed up by the earth. Could I get a new beginning in life? A do-over? I couldn't handle all of this hurt, abandonment, and strife. My unending optimism, which had been sustaining me through life, was being crushed by its counterpart: fucked reality.

John said nothing for a very long time. The three of us stared at each other, my eyes adjusting to the dark. Then he arose out of the bed and came over to tell me to go away. "Just go home, ok? You need to leave and go home." I turned around and did just that.

Abi was with Martin that weekend, so I was, thankfully, alone. I drank Gallo wine and cried like a suffering child. Two days later, on Sunday, I called Jessica to seek some much needed support, which didn't happen. "Jessica, he cheated on me," I said. "He had her in his bed with him, both of them naked. She, with her long blonde hair draped over her chest, trying to say hi to me like I was some damn buddy of hers. What the fuck am I going to do now?"

"I know," she responded. "He told Johnny about it. He feels awful. We invited him over here for a steak dinner, poor guy."

I became despondent. *She invited the cheater over for a steak dinner but didn't give a shit about the hurt I was feeling? What kind of friend is this?* I thought. With my self esteem bottomed out, I no longer cared. With no interest in caring about anything, I wanted to be swallowed up and gone. There was no way to make it on my own. I had to share expenses with someone, but it was difficult to find roommates for single parents. Losing this knight I believed in would be a devastating loss for me. Handling the situation pragmatically and moving forward was necessary. I wasn't sure if I had the ability, but I felt like I had no other option. The fear of becoming homeless and living on the streets kept me from leaving John. The thought of it freaked me out — I had a small child to care and provide for.

After many tears, talks, and endless promises from John never to cheat again, I stayed with him. Sadly, cheating leaves a lasting imprint, and things were never quite the same. I felt a hollow space where my trust should have been. Once more, thoughts besieged me of how insignificant I must be, that those who claimed to love me could turn around and hurt me to the core. *Or was karma paying me back? But for what? Having been an incorrigible teenager?* I carried so many conflicting emotions about my life so far, and I functioned with ongoing, consistent stress, lapping its way through my psyche.

40
SHERATON WINCHESTER INN

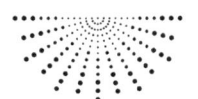

"Grow through what you go through" - Unknown

*J*ohn and I soon moved in together, and life became less heavy on me because I had someone to share expenses with. I enrolled in the Marietta-Cobb Vo-Tech school and entered the Secretarial Program through the Comprehensive Employment and Training Act (CETA). They offered a one-year training program in several fields, including secretarial, bookkeeping, and nursing. Tuition and books were all covered, and I received a monthly stipend for living expenses. The assistance helped me earn good grades and graduate the secretarial program. The school placed me in my first job as a secretary to the general manager and part owner of a

Sheraton Hotel. I thrived in this new environment and felt that life was finally on the upswing.

My new job came with a fresh cast of characters entering my life. Most notable were Christy Brendan, the accountant, and Mark Egan, one of the bookkeepers. Christy was half Japanese and stunningly beautiful. She could have easily modeled were it not for her petite stature. Her accounting skills were impressive, and I felt pride in her dominating in such a masculine line of work. She embodied all that I appreciated in other women. Strong, intelligent, glamorous, and street smart. Christy became a mentor to me, and I flourished under her guidance. She believed in my untapped abilities and helped me step up my game.

Mark became a great work buddy as we were closer in age. At 25, Christy had four years on me, where Mark was only 20. Mark had a crush on Christy and talked about her endlessly during our daily lunches together at the hotel restaurant, giggling and enjoying each other's company. He was my best buddy, and our friendship meant a lot to me. We ate in the hotel restaurant for free, a nice perk with the job. Mark was out for glamor and prestige in life, and, with someone like Christy at his side, he thought he could face no limits. However, Mark would never be the man that Christy wanted in a life partner. She unabashedly toyed with him, but would never commit to a man like Mark. She had higher expectations for her future.

One day during our lunch together, Mark approached me with a proposition. "Stephanie, I don't know quite how to say this, but will give it a try," he uttered. Sheepishly, he continued, almost whispering, "I've never had sex before." I was pretty stunned because he was a good-looking guy with an interesting personality. *He was shy, yes, but to that extent?* I was careful not to display any shock when he shared his big revelation. He explained he was hoping I would agree to an encounter with him at his apartment, to let him gain experience with sex. He knew I was living with John, and we'd been together for a couple of years by then. Apparently, it didn't bother him. I reflected on how this could help me, even the odds, so to speak, since I discovered John with the blonde bimbo. *Would I feel better if I evened that score?* I impulsively agreed. Within a couple of weeks, we arranged for me to go over to his apartment that he shared with his older brother. He was making sure his brother would be gone for several hours that Saturday. Whatever doubts I may have had about whether his virgin story was a crock of shit or, for real, were settled during our encounter. Mark was completely inexperienced, and it showed. I was patient. I felt vindicated. It was a great, albeit secret, retaliation for what John had put me through a couple of years earlier. Mark and I returned to our friendship with no further sexual encounters.

Another character who entered my life at work was the restaurant cashier Reba Blakely, whom Christy brought to the back office to work in bookkeeping with us. Reba was outspoken, flamboyant, very pretty, and slightly heavy. She was fun to be around, and we all enjoyed her humor. At Christmastime, Reba showered all of us in the office with individual, thoughtful gifts, each tailored so specifically to the recipient. I was pleased with and surprised by the classy contemporary water pitcher she chose for me.

Reba often volunteered to go to the bank for me, knowing I disliked taking the deposits there every day. It didn't bother her, and she was more than happy to help. Christy, Reba, and I made quite the team and even traveled together once.

Christy's friend, Joe Robinson, owned a time share condo in

St. Simons, Georgia, and she booked it for a long weekend so that we could go on a brief vacation together, and we were so excited. For our first night, we took forever getting all made up and dressed, so by the time we got out, it was close to 10:00. We had a good time eating at a restaurant and dancing at a club in the nearby hotel.

In 1979, the owners decided to sell the hotel. This was my first job in the work world, and I had grown to care so much about those I worked with. Rather than the dread my friends described, it was always fun to head to work. The prospect of finding a new job filled me with angst.

Christy lagged a couple of months behind on daily sales reports, so the owners pressured her to get caught up quickly, as the hotel sale required all the sales figures to be up to date. She trained Mark and me on how to process the daily reports to help her catch up.

One morning, as soon as I arrived at work, Christy called and asked me to come to her hotel room. It was the first time I'd ever seen Christy without makeup. Her usually flawless skin was ruddy, and her eyes sunken and dark underneath. It was obvious she was operating on little to no sleep. She was still so naturally attractive. "Hurry. Come in Stephanie, you need to see what I have uncovered," she said in a hushed tone, filled with alarm. Ignoring the strewn clothes and general mess around the entire room, I sat on the edge of the bed, looking over the spreadsheets and sales reports. Christy showed me where Reba had been taking money out of the daily bank deposits. She would take the deposit slips I prepared and write out a new one, decreasing the cash deposit by whatever amount she wanted to take that day. Then she erased my handwritten postings on the spreadsheet and changed the figures there, as well. Reba did not write like me, and her handwriting was much larger and loopier than mine. If not for that, it could easily look like I had done this. It sickened me to the core and scared the hell out of me as well.

In Christy's all-nighter she found Reba's stealing went back for months. It explained so much. I remember suspecting that Reba and her husband couldn't possibly be making enough money to buy the lavish gifts she showered on us over Christmas. She also spent fair amounts on herself, as well. Nice clothes, manicures, and nights out were common for her. Christy estimated that Reba had stolen over $5,000. Reba's theft and alteration of my spreadsheet figures left me shocked, speechless, and furious. She could have easily implicated me. My word and ethics were the only assets I had in those days, and they meant a lot to me. The possibility of Reba jeopardizing my good-standing made me livid.

Once Christy discovered these discrepancies, the scam was up. We plotted how to lure Reba to Christy's room on the pretense of going to lunch together, and once we had her in the room, we would confront her. I called her, and she bought the ruse, excited to be going to lunch just like old times.

When Reba arrived at the arranged hour, Christy let her into the room and then double locked the door behind her. Reba noticed and turned around to face her. I quickly positioned myself next to Christy by the door, in solidarity with her. I knew Reba might try to get past one of us but wasn't dumb enough to try to get by both of us. Instantly, she realized she was trapped, and crazy Reba surfaced. Reaching past us toward the door, we shoved her backward. She stumbled but caught herself, and yelled, "Let me out of here!"

"Shut up and sit down, dammit!" Christy admonished her. Reba reluctantly backed her way to the desk chair and sat down, arms crossed in defiance. My adrenaline surged as I realized how impactful this event could be. I knew keenly that the trajectory of this encounter with Reba could go in so many directions.

"I've been up all night, Reba, tracking down all the days and months that you have been stealing from this hotel. We are going to find you criminally liable, and you *will* be paying us back. Every damn penny! You have made an utter fool of me, and you tried to implicate Stephanie. You are as low as they come, and we won't ever forget this. Do you have anything to say for yourself?" Christy scolded her. By this time, Reba was in tears, hoping to garner sympathy, but neither of us was having any of it. We were pissed and demanded an explanation for this monumental betrayal.

"I don't know why I did it. I'm sorry." Reba murmured through her tears. It rang hollow. She didn't regret any of it, only getting caught for it. We could see she was scared but trying to hide it. Once past her initial shock, Reba realized she could jeopardize herself and clammed up. She wouldn't volunteer any more information, and the ordeal shut itself down.

Christy allowed her to leave, but not without first reprimanding her, "Reba, you will be paying for this. I'll have a total soon, and you can bet we will come and collect it from you or have you arrested for theft." Reba was still crying as she scrambled past us to get out the door.

I lost my so-called friend, Reba, that day but gained perspective that would stay with me, most particularly in future jobs dealing with money. For the sake of myself and my employers, I adopted good accounting protocols. I would never allow myself to be put into such a vulnerable position again.

As the chaos from Reba's theft came to its conclusion, the hotel's insurance company paid for the losses, totaling over $5.4K. The hotel decided not to press criminal charges because insurance covered the loss. Only the insurance company could now claim losses and recuperation from Reba, but they settled out of court for a fraction — $540. Reba got off with not much more than a slap on the wrist. Christy and I were livid, but there was nothing that could be done now. It was a travesty of justice, and the unfairness stuck with me.

41
RIDING IN CARS

"How we drive says so much about who we are." - S. Pleasant

Money was still tight. We made enough to get by week to week, but there were no extra funds for splurges. Whatever used car we had always needed repairs. Like my Saab sedan, three speed on the column, a can of oil in the gas tank before each fill up. I loved that car, and it was mine and paid for, but it often made my life miserable. It was always breaking down at the most inopportune time, and for a while I had to drive it while it flamed up during start-up. Once the engine turned over, the distributor cap caught fire because of a pin leak in one of the hoses. I started the car, then raised the hood and put the fire out with an old Army blanket I carried with me in the back seat. It was a nightmare if the wind was blowing. I always parked far away from other cars. On more than one occasion, someone nearby would come over in disbelief and want to help me put out the fire.

Not only did the cost of repairs keep me anxious, but there were many incidents that taken together earmarked me for a lifetime of uneasiness around vehicles. This was not my first encounter with fire and cars. At age 3, I sat in the back seat of our parked Cadillac and saw the front of the car on fire. Our driver, Carlos, quickly grabbed me out of the car and waited for the fire trucks to arrive.

Our castle home in Argentina was a corner property, and the main front door sat atop an elegant staircase that led to the first floor of the home. From the high vantage point, I often sat on the entry steps and watched what little traffic there might be on our street. Because they lacked stop signs, all neighborhood streets seemed to just yield to each other, and I often witnessed car accidents with both horror and fascination. Although I could see the imminence of the coming crash, I had no way of warning the drivers of their impending doom. Every pileup left me with scars. The worst one was a motorcycle coming down one street and a car down the other, slated to wreck, unseen by one another. When the crushing metals blasted their meeting, the biker was launched into the air. As he came back down, his legs landed in front of him in a seated position. He screamed out in pain and continued his agonizing cries as people rushed to his aid until an ambulance arrived and loaded him up. The incident left me unnerved.

On another occasion, I came across a severely wrecked car wrapped around a pole, still in place. The pole was there to prevent cars from crashing into the gift shop located in the heart of the curve, and it worked. As I approached my favorite little nearby store, the car was still there, untouched other than the removal of the body of the driver. The brain material, blood, skin, scalp, and hair all remained displayed exactly where they landed after the monumental crash. The horrid scene is still clear in the recesses of my visual memory.

One of my scariest car memories happened while returning home from the Glass family's outdoor luncheon party, where I experienced my first iced coffee at 11 years old and had an enchanting time. Their family chauffeur drove me home, but stopped at his house on the way to get some dinner. He left me alone in the backseat of his car and told me he would be right back. As he disappeared around the building of homes, his car, which was parked curbside on a steep hill, rolled backwards. I panicked and started screaming and banging on the window as I tried to open the back door. I was locked in. People nearby saw what was happening and scrambled over to grab the car to stop it from rolling any further. It took enormous effort, but they stopped it. I was terrified, crying, and the chauffeur, hearing all the commotion, came out of his house in disbelief as he unlocked the driver's side door and jumped in to push on the brake. He tried to play down the event to me, hoping I wouldn't tell anyone. An incident like this could get him fired and labeled as an undesirable hire.

Alberta was in the entryway, waiting for me, as it was later than she expected me back. My parents were upstairs in their beds and never heard about the incident, but Alberta did. I wrapped my arms around her soft belly and cried as I told her what had happened while she patted my back, reassuring me that I was fine and all was okay.

During my relationship with Bobby Smith in Atlanta, we

stopped at a gas station to fill up the tank and had an argument. Bobby slammed my door shut, and it caused the window to shatter all over me. I was stunned and sat there picking off shards of glass, some of which had nicked my arm. Bobby apologized and helped me step out from the scattered broken glass.

While living in Germany, my neighbor's five-year-old son, Joey, was hit by a car. He was crossing a nearby one-way street, and a car driven by a 20-something was going the wrong way. Decent German people that they were, they helped Joey by taking him to the nearest hospital, then returned to find Joey's parents and let them know what happened. Joey's mom, Gretchen, came banging on my door, crying, and as I answered, she urgently said, "Joey's been hit by a car and taken to a German hospital, please can you come with us to help translate?" I grabbed my purse, and off we went. The car accident injured Joey badly; he had a broken arm, open wounds, multiple scrapes, and bruises, and looked pitiful hooked up to tubes and machines that beeped rhythmically. It took weeks, but Joey made a full recovery and was outside playing again in no time. However resilient five-year-old Joey might have been, the experience shook me.

Another incident occurred when riding with Johnny Cantrell and Andrew Brady. We were rear-ended, and the car that hit us backed up quickly and spun around to get away. Johnny gave chase, and onto I-240 we went. The guy exited the highway at the last minute, and Johnny did not miss a beat, taking a right and heading the wrong way up the down-ramp. I was terrified. Once at the top, we drove in both directions but could not see where the car had gone until we noticed smoke in a grass clearing coming from the car's muffler. The vehicle went airborne as it came up the exit ramp and landed next to the trees in the corner median. Johnny pulled up next to the car and jumped out with a can of mace in his hand. He approached the vehicle and sprayed the 40-something man directly in the face. He howled as he got out of his car and rolled around on the ground. The irony of the incident is that Johnny and the man ended up becoming friends.

To this day, I don't enjoy riding in cars.

42
LANDING IN MEMPHIS

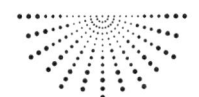

∽

"It's never too late to become who you want to be. I hope you live a life that you're proud of, and if you find that you're not, I hope you have the strength to start over." - Eric Roth

∽

I knew we needed to move away from Atlanta. John was getting so heavily attached to his excessive drinking and drugging lifestyle. I couldn't afford to lose him and end up alone again. We could make this work. I knew I loved him and felt he must love me too, on some level. A new environment would change the trajectory of our lives.

I spoke to an attorney about moving out of state with Abi. He said because Martin had only come to see her once in the past year and a half, we were free to leave without consequences. I wouldn't mind Abi not being influenced by Martin any further. Besides being a drunk, he dealt pot out of his house, which put Abi in dangerous circumstances whenever she stayed with him. He often would call to schedule a weekend visit with Abi, and excited, she would pack her little overnight bag and stand ready at the door for him to arrive. Sadly, many times, he never showed up. She would wait, dejected, and then she would finally accept he wasn't coming that day. It broke my heart and pissed me off simultaneously.

When we came home one evening and discovered that someone had broken into our rental house, we immediately decided that we wanted to move elsewhere. Atlanta crime was increasing exponentially. The violation felt from a break-in is visceral. I had several experiences in childhood that immediately surfaced and further prompted me to want to move away.

Burglars broke into the castle twice. Both break-ins occurred during the middle of the day while our dogs were locked up in the garage. I came home from school one day and discovered police officers all over our home. One crew was sprinkling black powder on everything, then sweeping it off delicately with a bushy dusting brush. I watched from a distance as the officers checked for fingerprints and looked for clues about our intruder. The drama sparked a lifelong interest in forensics and true crime books.

My older brother's coin collection was stolen, as was most of my mother's jewelry, including my father's gifts to her from Tiffany & Company. Mother was sad over the losses, and I found her crying softly, alone, shortly after the intrusion.

My mother was a member of a ladies' bridge group, and I always enjoyed when it was her turn to host. It meant fantastic food and even better conversations to overhear from my perch at the top of the staircase. I was privy to one particular story that enthralled me as I eavesdropped. "... It was midday,

Agostina was about to go down to her quarters for siesta time. They came up quietly and grabbed us from behind! Eye masks were placed over our eyes and gags in our mouths. Then they tied our hands behind our backs. They shoved us into the small guest bathroom and dared us to call out or make any noise," she recounted, with the same shakiness in her voice she likely experienced during the actual incident — a nameless trauma that one might expect in the tumultuous economic and political times of Argentina in the '60s. "We stayed so quiet. We did, I tell you. Agostina cried softly, and I tried to comfort her without making any noise. We could hear the robbers going through the house, turning out drawers and cabinets as they crept their way around to get whatever they were coming after," she added. "When they finally left, Agostina hopped to the window and yelled out, 'Ladrones! Ladrones!' to our neighbors' maid who was outside in their yard. She immediately found our neighbor Hans, to see if they could get into the house and rescue us." The robbers had entered through a back door that was left unlocked, and that is where Hans entered. "Thankfully, Hans was home, and as soon as he came over and freed us, the police were called. It was a harrowing experience, and we were so grateful nothing worse happened." That story left me with a healthy dose of fear, and I began keeping a double-edged razor on my nightstand while I slept.

Yeah, it was time to move on. Break-ins were serious threats, and this latest one left me feeling so unsafe. The search would begin for our next city to call home.

Memphis, TN, is where we ended up. After visiting Gordy there, we knew it was a setting we could enjoy living in. A smaller city, a few paces slower than Atlanta, and a brother and sister-in-law who I was sure would be nothing but a significant influence in our lives. Win-win. John, now trained as a heating and air installer, got a job at an HVAC company in Memphis. In November 1979, we said our goodbyes to Atlanta friends, packed up a moving truck, and off we went.

Adjusting to our new city was a smooth experience. We quickly settled into a routine that included a weekly visit with Gordy and Marie and their three children, Arnie, Karen, and Kelly. The weekly Sunday dinners later included Marie's sisters and parents, who moved to Memphis, and close friends from their military days, who transplanted there. It was wonderful to feel like part of a large family, something I hadn't experienced in a long time, if ever. Gordy had let go of my past, even though we never discussed it — part of our familiar family dynamic of not talking about family issues with anyone, especially other family members.

43
POT, MARRIAGE, AND BABIES

∼

"The choices we make dictate the life we lead"
- Eric M. Daniels

∼

When Abi was 5 years old, my mom came to Memphis to visit us and Gordon's family. She rarely visited, maybe every 6 years. We were excited to see and spend a day with her. She stayed at Gordon's house, of course; it was nicer and roomier than our small two-bedroom apartment. During her visit, while running errands with me and her grandma, Abi exclaimed from the back seat, "We just drove an upside-down pipe!"

"What did she just say?" my mother mused.

Swallowing hard, I mustered the courage to repeat what Abi

had said. My mother thought she was brilliant for pointing out the unique shape we traveled, while I, on the other hand, made a mental note that John and I needed to stop smoking pot. The final chapter of our hippie days was closed when we gave up our beloved marijuana. We owed it to Abi to provide her with a stable, normal home life.

After living together for five years, John and I finally got legally married and put on our own wedding. My parents chipped in for the invitations, a ham, and some fixings for the reception, and Mother brought her silver platters and crystal bowls to serve the various foods. We had a few close work friends and family attend. I borrowed a wedding dress from a co-worker and called it done. Precious Abi was our flower girl. John's two sisters were bridesmaids, and sister Ivette was maid of honor. John's dad and brother stood as groomsmen. We held the reception at the clubhouse of our apartment complex. A thriftier wedding and reception would be hard to come across. It was a considerable step up from the truck-stop diner.

Life trotted along as we met milestones, even if we did so behind our peers. Not bad for two blue-collar workers without college degrees. I worked as an administrative assistant and bookkeeper at a local Sheraton hotel, while John worked in the HVAC business, installing residential heating and cooling systems and learning sales. John had proven himself to be a good stepfather to Abi, and I was so grateful for his love and care for her.

In October 1981, we welcomed the birth of our son, Trevor. At 10 pounds, 12 ounces, and 24 inches long, he was enormous. The nurse who measured him showed me how long he was and then said, "I'm writing down 23 inches here. I hate for you to have to tell people you had a two-foot-long baby." It was love at first sight, every inch of him, and we were ecstatic to have our little family grow.

    I didn't want to go back to work and leave Trevor with a sitter, or worse, at a daycare. I longed to stay home and care for him myself, like I had with baby Abi. Luckily, our hotel manager had a large Catholic family of five children himself. He not only understood my situation but also created a new nighttime position for me. I would now help the night auditor during his 11 to 7 shifts. I worked from 10:00 pm to 2:00 am. It was a grueling schedule with a newborn, but the stamina of youth saw me through.

    After trying to catch some rest in the mornings, and while tending to Trevor, I also took care of a disabled young girl in the afternoons after school. Nikki, at nine years old and only 35 pounds, was oxygen deprived at birth and suffered from cerebral palsy. Unable to hold up her own head or body, she had to be carried everywhere or placed in her specially fitted wheelchair. She was tall and lanky and had beautiful long brown hair. Her mother's devotion to her was inspirational. Peggy was an avid seamstress and sewed all of Nikki's dresses and matching bows. She was always dressed beautifully. I would feed her a liquid dinner through a large bottle. Nikki's smile was all-encompassing, and there was nothing that made her laugh as much as hearing certain music, especially songs from the Smurfs, the cute blue gnomes that were the collectibles of rage during this period. Their high-pitched voices rang through the apartment as Nikki joined in by vocalizing loudly and grinning widely. Baby Trevor would bond with Nikki by singing along as well.

    I needed both part-time jobs to help cover the ongoing expenses we encountered, including sending our Abi to a private Montessori school and, later, to the private Country Day School. We knew a strong educational beginning would be invaluable and worth it, despite the financial strain. She thrived in those environments and would one day graduate as Valedictorian of her public high school.

44
THE FAM

"I've always put my family first and that's just the way it is."
- Jamie Lee Curtis

By the time Trevor was two, and Abi nine, we bought our first house. We qualified for special HUD financing as low income, first time home buyers. With a small loan from my brother, Gordy, for part of the down payment, it all became possible. We were ecstatic.

Six weeks after moving into our new home, I lost my job as a bookkeeper at a fine-dining steakhouse. A corporate franchise bought the locally owned and operated restaurant, resulting in all our layoffs. Frantic, I drew unemployment right away and began looking for another job.

One ongoing problem at the time was John's drinking and drugging. It really needed to stop. I had a moment of clarity with him and told him I couldn't spend my life with a drunk. Martin was abandoned for that reason. I damn sure would not live with another drunk alcoholic. Of course, I knew I couldn't afford to go anywhere alone. I had to hope he wouldn't call my bluff. He quit drinking cold turkey. Just stopped. I was so impressed. It was unbelievable how brave and strong he was to do such a difficult thing and make it look so easy. I was amazed and so thrilled to see John free from alcohol. He had embarrassed me publicly for the last time. No more yelling out in bars, no more injuries from him shoving me around or slugging me while I was driving his drunk ass home. Those days were over and I could not have been more pleased or relieved.

We went to visit John's family during holidays and at least one week in the summers. The O'Brien's lived in northern Florida, out in the countryside. Both of his parents worked at Raiford State Prison, his dad teaching CAD to prisoners and his mom, a surgical nurse at the prison hospital. They housed the infamous serial killer, Ted Bundy, there until his execution in 1989. Murph the Surf, another renowned jewel thief, was kept in their custody until he was released in 1986.

Trips to see John's family included the latest prisoner stories, which were always fascinating. During one visit to his family, we actually took a tour of the prison. We visited the shop where license plates were made, saw their cafeteria, and also explored the medical suite. In the operating room, John's mom, or Nanny as we called her, was showing us the surgical instruments and as she opened up one of the metal containers, a huge dead roach was floating in the antiseptic alcohol. Filled with criminals from all walks of life, the whole prison complex emanated an eerie energy throughout. You felt the prisoner's eyes surreptitiously follow you without even moving their heads.

45
ENTER OPRAH

"There is no greater agony than bearing an untold story inside you." - Maya Angelou

Oprah hit the TV scene, and it was life-changing for me. It was through her show that I learned so much about life, living well, and seeking your own spiritual, soulful path in life. I lived for her show and what I could learn from it. It was through Oprah that I opened the door to healing from my abandonment years earlier. I was slowly garnering more support for my 15-year-old-self. She deserved a voice and to be heard.

When we could finally buy our first VHS deck, I recorded Oprah's show every day. It was the highlight of my daily routine. After finishing chores and making dinner for the family, I unwound from the day by watching Oprah.

On one of those routine days, I was watching the show when I experienced a visceral response before I could even absorb what I was hearing. Oprah was talking about childhood molestation. What it is. What it did to you as a child. What effects lingered on into adulthood and the overall long-term ramifications of that experience. I felt for the sofa behind me, leaning back into it so as not to stumble over, my knees buckling, energy leaving my body. Hyper focused on her words, I came to the undoubtable conclusion that Daddy's Dooflicky game we played my entire childhood was not okay. I knew that game of his embarrassed me, even if I didn't know the reason. Of all our interactions, pastimes, and play, the Dooflicky game made me so uncomfortable. With honed repetition, his fingers would slide my panties aside and begin fondling my vagina. He also tweaked my nipples, which was equally embarrassing and uncomfortable.

I wasn't sure what to make of my newly found unearthing about a large part of my childhood. I sat on it. For over a year. Ruminating, wondering, bargaining, railing, and mourning, I tried to pack back down what I had unwrapped. It hurt.

John was so patient and understanding with me — up to and including foregoing any intimacy for however long I needed. He was my rock and supported whatever decisions I needed to make during the scope of this uncovering.

After a year, I decided that seeing a therapist and putting the memories to rest would serve me best. I found a psychologist that my insurance would pay part of, so we could afford it. I didn't want this bullshit to cost my family money unnecessarily. The psychologist I saw, Kathryn, was a young and kind looking woman and I felt comfortable with her, from the start. I shared my story and asked if she thought I was over-reacting to the childhood game and events that had transpired through my early years.

"Fine, Stephanie," Kathryn started. "Let's say you're right, that maybe there's nothing wrong with the Dooflicky game. After all, it wasn't violent. Would it be okay with you if John brought Abi into your bed and played with her like that?"

You could have wiped me off the floor. I forced down my rage as I responded quietly, "No."

"Well, then, why is it okay that it happened to you?"

Embarrassed to be crying in front of someone, I was speechless; the tears falling uncontrollably. *Why did I continue to regard myself as someone not deserving of common decency?* A significant tour of self-healing awaited me, one that is ongoing, and I am still committed to my journey of learning. I counseled weekly with Kathryn for three months, as long as my insurance would cover it, and took part in what therapy I could for that short period. I vowed to always strive for healing, health, and hope. I owed childhood Steppa and teenage Steph to right the wrongs inflicted on them, whatever that entailed or looked like, a promise for a future that began with healing the past.

Healing with Kathryn explained and answered many doubts. *Could this be a reason for behaving loosely sexually? Why I cared little about it but arrived at the young realization it was a tool to make men happy? Is this why I was a bedwetter until age seven? Was this why Linda Brewer was so upset when Lucy hazed her at summer camp and took off Linda's top? I jumped in to help Lucy when she asked me to, so was I complicit in mean girl behavior? Why was I okay with having sex at 14 years old? Why did I allow myself to be sold for sex?* Some questions eventually got clarification, while others, like, *Why did Mom allow this to happen in a bed right next to hers?* never got asked or, much less, answered.

46
VISTA IS BORN

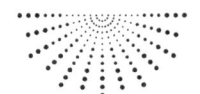

"Although no one can go back and make a brand new start, anyone can start from now and make a brand new ending."
- Carl Bard

One day in the Spring of 1988, John came to my workplace. I saw his truck pull up in the parking lot behind our offices. I was working as an admin and bookkeeper for Mr. Berg, a real estate developer in the area. He was a multimillionaire and a manic-depressive. Quite the combination — an entitled, miserable man. He put such dampers on my days that I often spent breaks in the ladies' room, blowing cigarette smoke out of the bathroom window and crying. His miserable soul damaged everything he touched. My co-worker, Isaac, had it even worse than I did, and listening to

Berg blast him endlessly was a constant source of anxiety and depression.

I set the office answering machine to catch the phone and dashed downstairs to see why John was there. I knew instinctively that it couldn't be anything good. My heart was racing and my palms sweating by the time I reached him. "I got fired from my job," he mumbled, as I climbed into the passenger side of his old, brown Chevy truck.

"What happened?" I murmured. It was inconceivable to me he could be without a job. *How would we pay our bills?* I knew my salary was not nearly enough to cover all of our monthly expenses. We hit all the usual milestones, but just barely, and way later than most. It was never easy. We lived week to week, paycheck to paycheck. Before I could sink any farther into the depths of distress, I realized I needed to buck up and see John through this fiasco. It would be our only hope. He couldn't descend into depression over this monumental loss. We needed him well and functioning.

"John, you've always wanted to start your own business. This is your time. Your moment. Let's do this now." I noticed his eyes gaze upward fleetingly as his body relaxed a bit. The stress of losing his job was going to take another route. With help and support, he could see this dream of running his own HVAC business finally come to fruition. It wouldn't be easy, but I knew we could do it. Life's newest challenge was upon us, and we were ready for it. I completely overlooked, or at least stashed away, that he had been stealing supplies from his employer and got caught and fired for it. It was crisis-mode time, and whatever it took, it took. This wasn't a time for second thoughts.

Vista Air Conditioning and Heating was born. John had his trials, but overall, he did pretty well and brought in some good money that first year. I followed the protocol that if you could put away your paychecks into savings for a year and live off the income from your business only, you were ready to quit your other job. I'd be so happy to finally escape that miserable haunt I was trapped in. A year later, in 1989, we were ready to be business partners full time. We would run his business as a sole proprietorship, and I would take care of all paperwork, monies, bookkeeping, payroll, banking, insurances, and taxes while John bid the jobs and did the actual work. It was great. We felt successful from the start. With virtually no overhead, we made a decent income from HVAC jobs.

47
FAMILY LIFE

〜

"The Lamps are different, but the Light is the same." - Rumi

〜

*A*bi went to college in town, and we enjoyed knowing she was nearby, even if we saw little of her. We raised our children to be independent, and seeing them thrive in college and high school showed us the fruits of our labor — they were forging their own paths, even if those paths had some bumps along the way. I was very proud of my children. They were good people.

Life became repetitive, but I enjoyed being able to count on the security of a schedule. I preferred the quiet of boredom to the frantic rhythm of stress. Besides work, my routine included going out to lunch and a movie date with my sister-in-law, Marie, and our friend Gracie, every Friday afternoon. The three of us had such a great time together, and we loved our girls' day out.

When Trevor wanted to learn karate, we enrolled him at the same dojo that his sister attended, where he thrived and earned his way through each belt rank. Watching Trevor work out, I was inspired by an elderly man in class, so at 40 years old, I signed up for training. It was a gratifying and enriching experience, and our school's competition team, which we were a part of, traveled to many southeastern states. The team placed first or second in their respective divisions at every national tournament we entered. Traveling together, we nurtured new, close friendships within our karate family. Beth was one of those treasured friends.

I spent a lot of time at the dojo because Trevor, now a black belt, started working there as an instructor when he was only 15 years old. Since I was at the karate studio anyway, I volunteered my way into a paid position tending the front desk and later, selling programs. Our head sensei, Richard, knew how to reach kids and made a real difference in their lives. He was great to work with and made the job so much fun. I loved my position there, and it was a great way to pay my way through earning my black belt.

Along with working at the dojo, I volunteered as a room mother and PTA board member. I really enjoyed getting to know my kids' teachers and their schools better.

I learned through our evangelical church that a local Catholic family had a son with autism and was looking for volunteers to help "pattern" their son, Jon. Patterning was the newest method being circulated to help children with autism. The premise was that children on the autism spectrum missed the crucial crawling stage and needed to emulate the pattern of crawling to re-wire their brains. I answered the call and began helping the Angostino's with 9-year-old Jon on a Saturday afternoon shift. It was my first experience with children on the spectrum, and I was so impressed with Jon's family. They were doing everything possible to improve Jon's quality of life, and their devotion to him was unmatched. We kept up the patterning for over a year, at which point the family ended the sessions, as they were not seeing the expected results.

One of my favorite volunteer jobs was dog walking at the local rescue shelter. Because we couldn't afford to have a dog, this was the next best option. Every week, I could meet and spend time with new dogs. It filled a void in me, and I felt a strong fondness for every dog I met and interacted with. This opportunity led to caring for the dogs of friends and family and developing a side business dog sitting.

Despite my resilience after my father abandoned me, I couldn't overcome feeling disposable. Low self-esteem lurked in the shadows and followed me everywhere. Volunteering helped me chase that darkness.

My negative mindset and lack of self-confidence hurt my prospects. I never felt like I lived up to my potential with only my eighth-grade education, GED, and secretarial certificate. I didn't believe in myself enough to aim higher. Since we were always struggling financially, college or advanced training wasn't an option. Unlike my siblings, Daddy wasn't there to pay my way.

Compared to the careers and marriages of my four siblings, I was the obvious black sheep. Since I was supposedly the smartest one of the bunch, it stood to reason, the expectations for me were probably pretty grand. None of those would come to be. *What a waste,* I often thought.

As my parents got older, they wanted to pare down their belongings and gave each of us our designated inheritance of family antiques. During that visit where we split up mother and daddy's furnishings at Gordy's house, some unbelievable news came to light for me.

While we were discussing furniture, inheritances, wills, and other related topics, I noted some unfairness directed my way, and Henry's wife Joan made an unexpected comment. She said, "Stephanie, considering you were the one who ran away from home, don't you think that's what you deserve?"

My mouth opened, my palms got sweaty, and my heart raced as I absorbed what she had just revealed. I was incensed. "What are you talking about, Joan? I never ran away from home. Daddy left me." The room fell silent. "Daddy left me at the Crisis Center in Atlanta when I was 15 years old," I further clarified.

Finally, Joan added, "I'm sorry, Steph. We didn't know. We were told by your parents that you ran away from home and ended up living with some woman in a big white house somewhere in the Atlanta area."

Gordy finally chimed in with, "We had no idea, Steph."

Wow, I thought to myself. *Not only did Daddy take me out of his will after he dumped me, but he told my brothers and sisters that I ran away! What an ass!* I felt awful for 20 years, believing my siblings saw me in the same negative light as my parents and were cool with them ditching me. Feeling "less than" for so long had crushed me, but finally hearing the truth revealed brought a sense of relief. It changed so much.

48
COCAINE

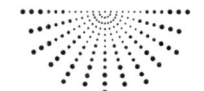

∽

"Your chaos is also my chaos." - Haruki Murakami

∽

On March 22, 2000, John walked into our kitchen after Trevor left for school and just said, "Cocaine." I wasn't sure I had heard him right.

"What's that?" I questioned.

"Cocaine," he answered.

"What? The song, or the powder? What are you talking about?" I asked.

"I'm addicted to cocaine. That's what's been wrong with me, what's been going on lately. It's why I'm seeing the counselor, too, besides the other things," he responded.

I could almost witness myself leaving my body. *Time to check out for a bit. Shit is getting heavy. No, go back. Deal with it. Pay attention. Fucking pay attention. Life-altering things going on. You need to pay attention and be able to figure this shit out.* I sat there dumbfounded, trying to be present in a situation that I instantly knew would be life-changing and mind-transforming. My body sank as I leaned onto one of our counter stools. My mouth went dry as my jaw clenched indiscriminately.

"I'm quitting today, so I just wanted to let you know. No more drugs, I'm ready to be clean and sober. I'll be joining a local AA group, too. They have a meeting tonight that I'm going to," he said.

Crisis averted, I thought quickly. *At least, most of it. He made a big mistake but is now correcting it, so we'll be okay. I can help him get past this. I'm the referee, the fixer. I can fix this hellish problem. Calm down and focus. Shit's going down, dammit.*

"John, is this what we've been spending our savings on? It's completely depleted and you keep telling me it's in jobs where you'll get paid back for it, but I never see any of it coming back in. Have you been spending it on coke?" I pondered out loud, not even trying to conceal the narrowing of my eyes and disdain in my tone.

"Well, maybe some of it," he stammered. "The jobs really are going to pay back our savings," he insisted.

"Exactly how much do we owe to our suppliers?" I questioned as I remembered fielding a couple of calls about past-due bills recently.

"I think about $2,000," he replied.

My heart sank to my toes. Not only were our savings depleted, but he apparently owed the HVAC supply houses $2K. Unreal. That was a month's worth of income for us. He was out of his mind. He was clearly not thinking properly, and it showed. His coke abuse desperately skewed his reasoning skills.

The silence was deafening as he went off to work, which at this point was selling HVAC for Sears. We were finally in a good place financially, or so I thought. He kept a few special Vista clients that he did side work for, and it was those that, for some reason, had our savings tied up. *All $15,000 of it?* It had taken refinancing the house even to have those savings.

I was still working part-time at the karate studio and went in that afternoon in a complete state of shock. I let Richard know how devastated I was by John's shocking revelation. He listened quietly, sat for a few moments, and then said, "Well, tonight is your fitness exam for your up-coming black belt test. Take all that devastation and turn it into power for your test tonight. I expect to see you here at 5:00 with the others, as planned."

That selfish fucker, John, had told me he was a drug abuser on the very damn day of my black belt fitness exam. A test that I had been working toward for four and a half years, training two to three nights per week. I had put that test date on the calendar months before, and we often mentioned it. Seriously, the worst possible day to drop that bomb about being a 47-year-old cokehead!

Our black belt fitness exam consisted of several hundred punches and kicks, hundreds of push-ups, and sit-ups, and also a two-mile, timed run at the very end. Grueling hours of physical work. The kind where you don't think you can possibly move one more limb and yet you have to. Your muscles scream at you, pain burning through tissue while your skin runs cold from the sweat.

I showed up at 5:00, as scheduled, though I was still in an alternate reality. Despite the devastation, I gave it my all. With every move, I let out bursts of pent-up anger, each "kiai" getting louder and more intense. I was punching and kicking out sadness and hate. But I made it. I passed it. I did it. I was so relieved. I had so much ahead of me, but that night, after three and a half arduous hours, I was a black belt in the making and so proud of myself. I cried myself to sleep, dispersing the pent-up bullshit of my crumbling life.

49
COPING

"Chaos is inherent in all compounded things. Strive on with diligence." - Buddha

The next few days revealed some painful truths. I was able to uncover that John owed the supply houses about $10,000 and our savings about $15,000. We were $25,000 in the hole — over a year's income. I felt sickened. *How could he? How can you claim to love your family and then put them in such peril over some hits of fucking coke?* I was so angry. *How damn selfish of him! How immoral of him. How embarrassing of him. How disrespectful of him. How hateful of him.* My sorrow turned to anger pretty quickly. Primarily because John had indeed gone to the AA meeting, but left early because, in his words, he was "not one of THOSE people." And that is how his "I'm quitting coke," started. Angry and disgusted, I didn't have time for pity, sorrow, or grief — those were for the privileged. I knew I needed to lock down some doors, starting with getting him removed from our bank accounts. In the early days of his disappearing from us, he went to a fairly nice motel and checked himself in using our joint Visa card. No need to allow him any further access to our money, as he would just continue stealing it to snort up his nose. I got to the bank that day and took him off of our joint accounts.

There was no one I could tell, so only Richard knew what was happening. I was completely alone in dealing with this situation. I knew our kids should be the first ones to know, ahead of everyone else. However, Trevor had only seven weeks left until he graduated high school and was scheduled to start at the University of North Carolina in Asheville in the fall. With finals and achievement tests coming up, he didn't need the burden of knowing his father was a drug addict. As long as I wasn't telling him, I wouldn't tell Abi either, as they should find out at the same time. That meant this was my secret to bear, and this path into the abyss would have to be traveled alone, for now

I tried not to burden John with my anger, either. I felt it might hurt his recovery, which I didn't want, but I still lashed out several times and said things I instantly regretted. Within weeks of revealing his addiction secret, I had a routine yearly exam with my gynecologist. Two weeks later, I received a notice that my Pap test had come back abnormal and I would need to get a retest done as soon as possible. I had never had an abnormal Pap, and it threw me off orbit even further. I fell into a black mood and decided John must have given me a sexually transmitted disease.

As soon as John got home, I waited for him to get his shower, change, and get into his recliner for a rare night home and some TV. I tried to stay calm as I asked, "Have you been cheating on me, John? I really need to know. This is a case where it could make a big difference to me. My Pap test came back abnormal for the first time ever. I'm really worried that I may have some kind of STD that you gave me. Please be honest with me. Please."

"No way, Stephanie. No damn way! You've gotta believe me. There's no way I would ever jeopardize our marriage or family. Never!" he exclaimed with ardent fervor.

"I'm just saying if there was ever a time to finally be honest, it's now. I need you to be honest. Since we're not staying together anyway, it won't make any difference if you tell me the truth in this case."

"How can you think such a thing, Steph? No way. I'd never betray you and that you even think I could, hurts me deeply. It really does. Why would you believe such a thing about me? How could you?"

Unable to prove anything otherwise, I felt belittled for letting myself think he would cheat on me. He was supposed to love us all so much.

The worst time I snapped at him was when he said, "I want to take the .22 out in the back yard and shoot myself."

"You don't have the balls to," I retorted. The words stung my mouth on their way out, and I instantly felt horrible for having said them. I apologized immediately. Over and over. I knew he'd never let me forget that comment. It terrified me he might carry out his threat, and I'd never forgive myself if he took his own life, so I hid the .22 rifle.

I already carried enough guilt about Bobby Smith's suicide. At 21 years old, Bobby took his life by blowing his brains out with a rifle. His funeral was another "first" for me. I had a really difficult time coping — wondering if the events that transpired between us and my father, just a few years earlier, contributed at all to his decision to give up on life. He supposedly left a note, but none of us friends were privy to it. His mother kept it to herself, whatever it said. Bobby had always been tormented about being adopted. He often wondered out loud why his birth mother didn't want him. *Did that contribute to his checking out from life?* I won't ever know. I knew this event solidified a hatred of guns.

John would come home really late, always claiming it was a job that made him late, and each story, reason, and explanation was as believable as the next. It was easy for him to come up with plausible excuses, especially because of his line of work. He stayed out late every night.

The days ran into each other like a blurred storm. Each one brought more bad news as fast as I could stomp out the previous undesirable challenge. It really was like a game of whack-a-mole. I closed out our joint Visa and put the debt onto a card of his own. His debt, he could own it. USAA, a provider of services for armed forces members and dependents, was incredible — a lifeline for me during this awful time. They allowed me to open my own Visa with a $5,000 limit, holding only a part-time job. The next time I saw John, I let him know what was going on. He didn't care. His only goal in life was to get more coke. I had him cash in his IRA, worth about $13,000, so I would have a means to pay for the mortgage each month. Sears was another champion in my life. They kept him on the payroll and offered all the help they could. The support he got from them was so encouraging.

50
LIFE WITH AN ADDICT

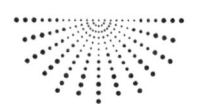

∽

"We march like fools in the parade of chaos." - Zao

∽

Trevor's high school graduation finally arrived. He did well on all of his tests and graduated with honors. I was so proud of him, but dreaded the news he would absorb soon. The family arrived for graduation, and we all sat together in the bleachers. The only person not there was John. He finally called and said he was sitting in another area of the vast stadium. The family sensed something was wrong, and I knew that I would have to reveal to them what was going on soon. Outside after the ceremony, I saw his truck drive by us without a glance from him. He was going fast and seemed fixated.

I insisted that John be the one to tell Trevor about his addiction and that he do so in my presence. I knew his capacity for lying reached far beyond what I thought possible.

After days of not knowing where he was, I called to check on him. He answered the phone in a fake jovial tone. "I'm working down in Tunica, Mississippi, today," he said, interrupted by his phone beeping in. "Hold on." He clicked his phone over and unwittingly put me on a three-way conversation. I stayed deathly quiet as I listened to what unfolded.

"Mendenhall and Park. What's your number?' asked a rough, low voice I didn't recognize.

"Three," John answered. He then clicked back over to me, or so he thought.

"So, what did you need?" he asked pertly.

"Who was that you were just talking to," I asked trying to mask the trembling sweeping through me.

"Oh, it was Nathan Vex," referring to an HVAC friend of his he worked with.

"Stop lying to me, John. You put me on a three way call and I heard your entire conversation."

Click. The call went dead. He hung up on me. I ordered the phone records for his personal cell phone, and I tracked his calls, so I noted the date and time. It sounded like a drug buy, and I wanted to know for sure who this was and the purpose of the call. It was this incident that showed me the depth of his lies and his capacity to execute those lies with the veracity of a judge.

On the Saturday morning after Trevor's graduation, I had John explain to him what was going on. Trevor and I sat around the kitchen bar while John stood in the doorway, as he managed to eek out, "I need to let you know that I've been abusing cocaine. It's been going on for a while, and I'm determined to quit and will be going for help. In fact, I'm working with Sears to figure out a treatment plan. Everything will be fine, I just needed to let you know what was going on. I'm very sorry, Trevor." He left the house teary-eyed, presumably to go to work. Trevor said nothing. He was as shocked as I had been months before him, and I allowed him the space he needed to process the situation.

Abi had confronted me after my birthday party in March about something being wrong with John. "He's sniffling, constantly. It's like he has snorted something. He's all jittery and acting funny." I knew I couldn't lie to her, so I said nothing. "I think he is snorting cocaine. Are you aware of that?" she persisted.

"Yes," I responded, not wanting to lie to her. "He's using cocaine, but you can't say anything to anyone, please. Trevor needs to get through exams and graduation, so please don't say anything to anyone. We're dealing with it. Dad's going to go to treatment." She was appeased for the time being.

During the chaos and before Trevor's graduation, I earned my black belt. Abi and one of her friends showed up to see me test for it and to watch Trevor earn his second-degree black belt. It felt so good to have them and my precious granddaughter, Siren, supporting us from the sidelines. John showed up at the very end, trying to look good for his kids, not for my benefit. I knew how he operated by then. He wasn't the man I thought I knew, no; he was a very different creature. I felt an immense loss for the man and life I thought I had.

It was time to let Gordy and the family know. I dreaded this so much. They loved John and treated him well, as he did them. We all bonded together, a tight-knit group, and this news was going to shatter them. It went against everything they knew and loved about John. He was the rock. The one who could tell you if your kids were lying to you. The one who would know if your kids were up to trouble or hanging out in the wrong places. The one who would take your kids under his wing and treat them like his own. He was a wonderful uncle, and when he was present, a great dad. All of this was called into question. How can you live a constant lie and yet be real for the people you love and who love you? It doesn't work. It can't. I lost confidence in what was real and what wasn't, and depression set in to stay.

The family still got together every Sunday at my brother's house, and on one of these Sundays, I shared the distressing news with them. I choked my way through as I explained, "John let me know in March that he's been abusing cocaine. I've wanted to tell y'all, but I couldn't 'cause our kids deserved to know first. With Trevor facing finals and graduation, I couldn't let him know until school was over. So, this is my first chance to share it with you." They cried along with me. The news was raw, and, as expected, they were all distraught and upset. I was currently past the anger and into pity mode, but I wanted my life back. It had been unexciting, but I appreciated the pace and security created by a routine. The current chaos of our lives brought a consistent level of anxiety and stress, with an overwhelming feeling of being perpetually on edge.

John went to the inpatient treatment facility, Lakeside, but only lasted there one night. He said it wasn't the right place or treatment for him. Once again, he identified himself as too special to be with the others he encountered in rehab. He couldn't see himself as "being one of them." I was crushed that he didn't go through with it.

He no longer stayed at the house with any consistency, and we never knew where he was at night. He only came around to steal valuables to sell for coke money. With no access to our accounts, he resorted to stealing and pawning and came to the house when he knew I was at work. I changed the locks, so he entered through the garage door. I changed the garage door code, and with that entry blocked, he would have to resort to breaking a window or kicking down a door if he wanted to get in. The night I changed the garage code, John called me at the studio while I was working out in a class. Richard answered the phone and motioned to me it was John, as he said, "hold on," and handed me the phone.

"You should not have done that," a low, angry voice came through the earpiece. I barely recognized him. It was like an alien being had taken over John's body and voice. A distinct tremble went up and through my sweaty, exhausted body.

"What are you talking about?" I responded, knowing full well what he was referring to.

"You locked me out of the house," he said. "It's still my house, too."

"John, all you do when you come over is steal things and then pawn or sell them. Sober John wouldn't do this crap or approve of what you're doing. I'm going to do my best to protect our property while you go through this crazy shit."

"You better let me in to get my stuff."

"Sure. Come by whenever you want, just let me know ahead of time and I'll be there to let you in," I said in the friendliest voice I could muster. He hung up, as I was letting him know that his call was scary and not appreciated at all.

The encounter left me rattled and actually scared of the unknown. *Who knew what this John was capable of? Would he physically hurt me?* As soon as I got home that night, I saw my next-door neighbor outside and confided in her what was going on. I asked her if she heard me screaming for any reason, to call 911 right away. She confessed she had a coke problem in her college years but had quit while she was still fairly young. She assured me she would keep an eye on the house. I appreciated that more than she knew. That night, I didn't just lock my bedroom door, I also placed a chair under the door handle. I felt like I was part of a cop show, barricading myself in my bedroom, trying to feel safe enough to sleep. What a rare gift sleep had become. There was no quieting my monkey mind. It stayed reeling 24/7, while the chaos kept burgeoning.

The next time John came by the house, I was there. He talked to me in that same dark, aggressive tone. I tried to get back to my room to lock him out, but he stayed right on me.

"Why did you go and do that?" he questioned, angrily. "Why would you lock me out of my own house? I'm free to sell or pawn any of my stuff if I decide to. You can't stop me." On and on he went, as we walked back toward our bedroom. I was scared and truly afraid he was going to physically hurt me. I jumped on the bed, onto my back, with my feet up, bent at the knees, ready to kick his throat if I needed to.

"What's wrong, scared I'm going to hurt you?" he taunted. "Why would you even think that?" he said menacingly as he leaned in toward me, stopping only within inches of my face as his spittle landed all over me like tiny shards of glass. "Do you really think that?" He had clearly lost his mind. The torment of this guy threatening me was excruciating, and I couldn't fathom who he was. I said nothing, nor did I answer any of his rhetorical questions. Reading about addicts taught me the pointlessness of arguing with them, especially while they're high. I also didn't want to take any chances of escalating the already precarious situation I found myself in. It was surreal. He finally backed down, grabbed some items from his dresser drawers, and stormed off. I assumed he took his grandfather's valuable pocket watch to go pawn next.

51
STEALING AND SELLING

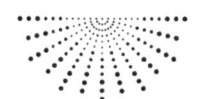

"If you do what you've always done, you'll get what you've always gotten." - Tony Robbins

Of all the things John took from the house, there were several sentimental items that I was sad and angry about losing. My wedding ring set, the sterling silver rings from Tiffany & Co. my father had given me over the years, and the Seiko watch John gave me for Christmas. I knew I'd never get replacements, and I lamented the loss deeply. He sold off an antique banjo that a client had given him years ago. It was worth thousands of dollars, and he promised it to Trevor, a talented self-taught musician. I watched in utter disgust as an older man arrived at our house to pick up the classic banjo and pay $300 for it. Knowing the money would go up his damn nose just irritated me to the core. What a colossal waste. I was now charged with protecting our house, our cars, our money, our mail and, most importantly, our son, my daughter, and granddaughter from the ravages of an addict I no longer knew. It was a monumental task and one of the heaviest burdens I ever had to deal with. Because of the constant fear and lack of good sleep, I stayed in a perpetual state of crisis and exhaustion — my mouth dry, lips parched, and my stomach in turmoil.

I could not protect Abi from him. He took the window air conditioning unit from her little rental house and never replaced it, as he told her he would. She and Siren stayed hot for a while, until she saved enough money to buy another used unit. It was a new low for him.

One of the hardest people to tell about John's addiction was my father. He reacted as I suspected he would. Irish-born paranoia mixed with military pragmatism and wartime anxiety. His law degree came in handy for him and anchored me to my already heavy load. He often called me at 6 a.m., just as I drifted off to sleep, if it was a night designated for some actual downtime. Groggy and exhausted, our dialogue sent me over the edge.

"Stephanie! What are you doing about protecting your house and car? You DO know, don't you, that if they find any drugs on him, they can confiscate his assets. That would include your house and any vehicles you own. It doesn't take much, just a little bit of cocaine powder and you will lose everything. You'd end up on the streets with no home. What are you doing? Are you aware of this threat?" On and on he would go, calling at least every day, if not several times a day with his latest worst-case-scenario he was thrashing around in his worried mind.

"Daddy, I am taking care of protecting our assets, please

don't worry. You worrying doesn't help me at all. I need support through this ordeal, not added pressures. I've spoken to an attorney who told me to 'quit claim deed' the house into my name, so I've done that. All joint accounts we've had, are closed. He's been removed as beneficiary of any insurance policies we have. The cars are already in mine and Trevor's names only. The truck is in his name, and I'll leave him that. I don't want to be mean or vindictive. He's sick, daddy. He's sick in the head and addicted. I've scoured our house from one end to the other and there are no drugs here. He also swears to me that there are no drugs in our house, and I believe that. Any drugs would've been used right away, not stashed away somewhere. I've had him cash in his IRA of about $13,000, so I'll have funds to pay bills with. I've got the house up for sale by owner and will get an agent right away if it doesn't sell in a month. It would help me a lot if you would stop calling so early. I can't sleep at night, Daddy. My mind won't stop racing and I'm scared here in this big house, all alone. If I do get any sleep, it's between 5 a.m. and noon. I can sleep if there is daylight outside. It feels safer to me. Daddy, please don't tell Mom what is going on. I don't want to burden her any and I know her health is poor right now." Adamant about the last part, I hadn't forgotten the vow I made to never hurt my mother again. No, she didn't need to be worrying about me with her own health in such a precarious state. At 85 years old, her Parkinson's disease and arthritis had ravaged her body down to a barely movable skeleton.

52
THE COUNSELOR

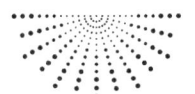

"Your words mean nothing when your actions are the complete opposite." - Unknown

During one of his now rare stops by the house, John said his counselor wanted to meet with me. All three of us. My blood ran cold. Sure that John blamed me for his addiction, there was no way I would subject myself to that hurt, and I was in no mood for it. "Why?" I asked. "There's no point as far as I can tell. You've chosen this path, and I can't do anything to stop you or help you. There's no point in all three of us meeting."

"No, no, you don't understand. He wants to see if you're willing to stay with me while I get help for this problem I'm having. That's all. Just to see if you'll stay with me long enough to get well. That's it."

"I've told you from the start that I'd do that. I'll stick by you until you're well enough to start off on your own again. I'll be here for you," I replied.

The third time John asked me for a meeting with him and his counselor, I finally agreed. I'd buck up and take whatever blame they wanted to throw my way. The meeting was arranged, and within a week, I found myself in the counselor's waiting room, witnessing John's inappropriate flirting with the receptionist behind the glass-fronted counter. Their exchange of knowing grins sickened me. He returned her fawning gaze and toothy smile.

"John, I'd really appreciate it if you would avoid flirting with another woman while I'm waiting here to meet with your counselor. What kind of man does that? It disgusts me," I spewed quietly.

"But I'm not flirting with her. I just know her from coming here, that's all," he retorted as he smiled at her.

More bullshit. I realized at that moment that nothing would make me stay with him. Even if he got clean, the fact that he was such a constant flirt with other women made me completely distrust him. I was convinced that he was cheating and lying to me in more ways than one.

Entering the counselor's office, I was convinced that he would blast me from all sides for not being "nice enough," or "good enough," for John. *Or maybe about the months I could barely have sex with him because I was in counseling over my father's molestation. Who knew what they might come up with?*

I kept my trembling fingers intertwined so they wouldn't be visible to John and his counselor, Carl. I sat quietly, waiting for one of them to talk.

Carl broke the silence. "Stephanie, we aren't here today to assail you in any way. In fact, quite the opposite. You've suffered greatly from John's indiscretions, and you have every right to be angry and ready to leave him and this marriage. However, in the interest of John getting better, he wants to know if you'll stick by him while he gets treatment and help for his addiction problem. Would you be willing to stick around long enough for that to happen?"

"Well," I answered, "I let John know from the beginning that I'd stick by him as he got better, yet all he has done for the past two months is go to some kind of help or treatment and then leave before it's over. I'm sick of the disappointment I continually face, on top of the messes of daily reality I deal with. It's too much. I don't even know who this John is, to be honest. He's not the John I thought I knew, and the John I knew wouldn't tolerate this kind of behavior from anyone, much less, a family member."

"I am afraid there is probably a lot about John we don't know and may never know," Carl said quietly. A hint of pessimism sneaked out with his soft voice. It was one of those memorable sentences. One that grabbed my attention for later rumination and dissection. Those words would come back to goad me more than once.

"I'll stick by him and give him whatever support he needs, but he's got to get serious about getting better. No more getting our hopes up and then not following through."

"I can do that," John finally uttered, as his first response to anything. "I'll make sure I get to treatment and all my AA meetings."

We left that meeting on a high note, feeling like John was going to really do it this time and that he'd finally get clean and sober. I didn't agonize over John flirting with the receptionist.

Instead, I focused on his recovery and what that would mean for us as a family. Sears was still sticking by him and if he could just get clean, they would keep him on in his sales capacity. We had so much to lose if John couldn't get sober. Please dear God, heal him. Heal us. Please.

Maintaining a positive attitude was my goal. I operated as though John was going to get clean and continue his successful career with Sears and Trevor would go off to college in NC, as planned. I would be free to pursue a career in karate. Richard looked to open more studios and assured me that one of those could be mine to run one day. Many opportunities were coming our way. I prayed we were ready to recognize, receive them, and make them flourish.

53
MORE MYSTERIES SURFACE

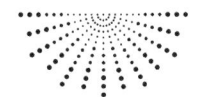

"Recovery Is an Acceptance That Your Life Is in Shambles and You Have to Change." - Jamie Lee Curtis

There was only one showing of our house when I listed it for sale by owner. She was a drug addict looking in our cabinets for pain medications. I confronted her, and she got mad and left.

I found the agent who sold our last house and ushered us into this one. Karen was good, and I liked her friendly style and confident attitude. She gave me more tips, including forbidding me to smoke cigarettes in the house anymore — garage only. That was a tough one for me. I spent my nights at home crying, smoking cigarettes on a step stool in the garage. I was exhausted and fighting hopelessness with all I had left in me.

Time seemed to fly by with the intensity of the whack-a-mole life getting fuller and more defined. I was in touch with Patrick, John's younger brother, who I'd always been very close to. Patrick and I exchanged John stories, and I discovered this wasn't John's first foray into the drug world. Apparently, when I was so proud of John for quitting drinking cold turkey, he wasn't worthy of the praise. John just picked up pot smoking again. From there, our family doctor apparently prescribed painkillers to him for his back problems, and he had long since become addicted to them. Years. It threw me back into shock mode once again. John abused drugs for years, not the eight months he tried to pass off on all of us. His cocaine addiction had been going on for at least two years. He mastered hiding it. When I confronted him about the white spots all over his dark green pillowcase, he claimed it was sinus troubles, a runny nose from allergies, and I bought it. It made sense to me. I was dealing with seasonal allergies and was receiving allergy shots for three years of a five-year plan. So, all the time that I spent praising John for his sobriety was a big farce. Patrick helped guide me in understanding this dark world of John's. His help also kept me safe.

I ordered more copies of John's cell phone bill for the past six months. To get these copies, I falsified verification to the phone carrier, my naturally deep voice claiming it was from "John." I pored over them and started making connections. I determined two drug dealers' phone numbers based on their pattern of use from John. The number he called most often was the one I dialed.

"Three," the male's voice said roughly, after a single ring.

"Quit selling drugs to my husband, John O'Brien," I seethed. The dealer hung up. Within a few hours, John called and started threatening me on the phone.

"You'd better leave well enough alone. Don't be calling any of the numbers from my phone. You don't know these people. They're capable of anything and I can't promise your safety amongst them. Don't go down this road, Stephanie, it's one you can't turn around from. Just stop it, do you hear me?" he yelled.

"I'll do whatever it takes, John, to see you get sober," I responded.

The next time his brother Patrick called, I asked him about John's threat. Patrick said it was bullshit. John was only worried about messing up his connections. If this dealer deemed him too hot, he might cut him off. I was relieved to know I wasn't in any danger, yet sick at the same time. John's calls showed he was using coke every day. Multiple times a day.

The cell phone records also revealed several numbers that were called a lot, but those could be jobs he was on, so I ignored them. I started piecing together what transpired after certain events and found answers to many questions I had amassed. For one, after my niece Kelly's wedding and reception, which lasted well into the night, John claimed he had to go on a call for a family whose heat was out. It was plausible, but quite a stretch. Sure enough, from Kelly's reception, he contacted one of his dealers and went off to buy and use coke. He didn't show up at home until the wee hours of the morning. I also wondered whether he was high or needed a high when we met at the attorney's office to settle our divorce agreement and sign papers. Once again, he contacted his dealer right after that appointment, leaving me to surmise he was sober and jittery for a fix early that day. I made a copy of the phone bills to stash at work, so John couldn't find and destroy them.

My boss, Richard, connected me with a guy who could access local pawn shop records. We used John's social security number and printed out all the items he pawned around the city. The printed pages stacked about two inches high. I was astounded. I was barely aware of the shitload of stuff he took from our home. The list included all my jewelry and many pieces that weren't mine. *Who else was he stealing from? Friends? Girlfriends? Was he burglarizing homes?* The mystery deepened. A part of me didn't want to uncover any more. I was already overloaded as it was.

54
DIVORCE, DEATH, AND DESPONDENCY

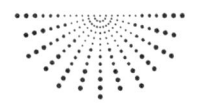

"Addiction doesn't kill the addict. It kills the family, kids and people who tried to help!" - Anonymous

I shared only a few of my findings with Trevor, because I didn't want to overburden him while he prepared for college. I was hoping college would give him a fresh start, a chance to move on and leave his past behind.

When my best friend, Beth, from karate realized that I was taking Trevor to college alone during this madness, she took off from work to help. I was shocked anyone would do this for me, and her deep caring reached my heart. I wept with gratitude.

We bought a used Ford Explorer for Trevor to take to college with him, and I planned to keep the minivan. However, because of our new circumstances, it was no longer affordable to insure Trevor in the Explorer. We left the respective vehicles as they were. We took both cars to North Carolina, Beth in the Explorer with me halfway and riding with Trevor in the minivan the other half, keeping us upbeat and positive.

Once in North Carolina, we had no time for anything but to get Trevor to campus and in with his group of newbies. Beth and I hugged him goodbye and promptly burst into tears before we could get back to the car. Crying our hearts out, it was such a bittersweet moment. I was once again alone in life. My son would never live at home again. He was free. Free of the burdens we brought on him. May he continue his life in another vein and flourish ad infinitum. My job as a parent now was to let him fly free and protect him all I could from the residual ravages of his once stable family and home.

The Explorer broke down on our way out of town. Beth had to be at work the following Monday morning, and we could not stay in Asheville for another night. The mechanic fixed it by 5:00 in the evening. We hit the road and made it back to Memphis around midnight. I could not express to Beth enough how much she meant to me, how much her accompanying me touched my soul to the core. I don't know that I could have endured the grueling experience without her. My first night alone in the big house scared and saddened me. It took me hours to fall asleep. Every house noise became an intruder, likely John, coming to get me. His darkness permeated our house, filling me with distrust and fear.

The days got blurry, as did my body. While shopping in a large craft store, I suddenly felt weak, queasy, and trembly. Unsure of what was happening, I felt as though I might faint at any moment. I sat on a display bench and bent my head down between my knees to get blood to my head. I felt embarrassed, but it worked. Whatever happened to me seemed to drift away, and I was so grateful I hadn't fainted. I began experiencing these episodes of blurred vision and feeling like I was going to faint more often, and some episodes were quite scary.

Once, on our way to a karate tournament in Nashville, with a van-load of teens, I had to pull over on I-40 and get out of the driver's seat. My palms were sweaty, and my eyesight seemed to narrow to a pinpoint, and I had no idea what was happening or why. Without missing a beat, Beth got out, walking around to the driver's seat. She never asked what was happening. I quietly murmured to her, "I think I need something to eat," as I didn't want to scare anyone. She got off at the next exit and pulled into a McDonald's for food. Again, that was the kind of friend Beth was. We could convey and communicate without words. She was a priceless jewel in my life, especially during these really punishing times. I later came to learn that these episodes were panic attacks, brought on by anxious situations or stress. My intuition heightened again from the stress of fraught reality.

Our divorce was finalized, and John didn't show up in court to contest it or even just to see it through. He was out high somewhere, no doubt. I was pretty anxious and felt so alone as I sat in front of the judge and answered his questions, which thankfully, were few. The divorce decree that John agreed to called for him to support Trevor through college by paying for his education and for medical insurance coverage and a stipend to live on. He was also due to help me financially until I could get on my feet and find a full-time job, or go back to school and get trained for a new career. We would never see the money promised to us. Trevor would end up paying his own way through college, taking out student loans, and working various jobs for spending money as well. His steadfast self-sufficiency was a godsend to me. I was so grateful to have a son with an old, compassionate soul.

My mother's health steadily deteriorated, and it saddened me so. I needed her, and yet couldn't share my circumstances because of the stress it could cause. I stuck to the promise to my brother and kept the phone calls with my mom positive. While I gave my father the complete update and rundown on the phone one afternoon, I learned he had put my mother on the other phone line. I was devastated. *How dare he do this against my specific request for him not to? And to what end?* My poor mother mustered up her very last, halting words to me, "Stephanie, you'll be alright." She died less than a week later, two days before my flight to go see her. I sobbed for days. *How could Daddy have done this to Mom? To let her last knowledge of her youngest child be such sad, detrimental news? What a selfish prig*, I thought. I was also furious with John, that he would cause us all this much pain and suffering and let my mother leave this world with so many unknowns. I couldn't help but feel that addiction was such a selfish disease. All about feeling good, all the time, regardless of the consequences and effects on so many others.

With the weight of losing my mother on top of all the other pain and loss I was going through, it felt as if there was no hope or relief in sight. As a positive person, it was devastating for me to feel so consistently despondent and alone. Getting through each day was a challenge that I dreaded instantly upon waking. My escape into slumber or heartfelt daily tears was my only means of releasing pent-up pain and anger. Physically drained, I laid down in bed or on the sofa any time I could.

55
PAMELA SEEKS ME OUT

"Don't expect her to play her part if you have other women auditioning for her role." - Unknown

In December 2000, five months after John had to be locked out of our house, I ran into a client of his at the movie theater. I was with Marie and Kelly for one of our Friday afternoon movies and lunch. A curvy, blonde woman approached and said she recognized me, that I was Stephanie O'Brien, married to John O'Brien, and we had met before. "Yes," I recalled. "You came by the house to help with selling it by owner."

"That's right," she responded. "How has that gone?"

"Not well," I answered. "We finally listed it with Catherine

Thompson whom we used to sell our last house, but so far, no one has put in an offer."

"Please call me, Stephanie, here's my card. I have some information to share that may be of interest to you."

The statement totally puzzled me, but I said I would call her soon. I vacillated about whether or not I actually would. Something about her seemed off to me. Marie, who had heard the entire exchange, felt the same way — something seemed really odd about the whole verbal and nonverbal exchange. The unspoken language needed further translation.

A few days passed, and I caved. I wanted to know what Pamela, the real estate agent, knew about John. I felt an urgency to find out more. Once I called her, I took a backseat and let her lead the conversation. I kept pretty quiet as she carried on about how well she knew John. "Stephanie," she started out cheerily, "thanks for calling me, I've really wanted to talk with you about John. He and I became pretty close friends over the past years, actually, since the early 90s. We met when someone recommended him to me for HVAC work I needed done right away on a house I was listing for sale. I started using John for all my heating and air conditioning needs. We grew close over time, and I got to know him well. When I heard he was out on the streets doing drugs, I immediately thought about you and wondered if he was trying to blame you for his plight and addictions. It's the kind of thing I know he'd do."

"Hmm, yeah," I murmured.

"Stephanie, John is very selfish and self-centered. He has an entire group of friends that he hangs out with that you don't know of. Most nights when he told you he was working late; he was actually out partying with his friends. I think you may have at least heard of one or two of them, like Nathan Vex and Trent Facet," she paused.

"Yes, I know those two guys," I interjected.

"They all drink, smoke weed, snort coke and share pills — mostly pain meds. He really did live in fear of you finding out about his *other* life," she continued, "sure that you'd leave him if you discovered his lies."

I struggled to keep pace, frantically scribbling down her confession.

"Do you know why he always asked you about what movie you were going to see on Friday's and which theater you'd be going to?" she asked. Before I could answer, she continued, "He wanted to make sure he wouldn't end up at the same theater as you. He went to the movies every Friday afternoon, like you."

Imagine that, I thought, as I quickly recalled that *I indeed would give him our exact plans for every Friday excursion with Marie.*

"Stephanie, let me share a moment with you that has come back to haunt me these days. John was over at my house, working on my HVAC system. My sister called and was telling me a story about catching her new boyfriend in a lie, and I was musing about it with John, afterward. He paused, looked at me rather seriously, and said, 'Once a liar, always a liar.' That really struck me." It resonated with me as soon as she uttered it.

"Do you remember when you started taking Spanish classes? He was so afraid you were preparing to leave him. That was his biggest fear all the time — that you'd be leaving him."

I sat back in utter shock. *There was no way this woman knew John so well and had not been a mistress. For one thing, John was too selfish with his time and attention. He wouldn't spend it with someone who wasn't giving him something in return for it.* But I let her carry on and dig herself into a huge hole. She all but said he has a mole on his penis. The revelations were so telling. She concluded by sharing that she knew he was on the streets these days, because he had called her recently, trying to convince her to let him stay at her place. She turned him down and told him to go get help.

I got off the phone with her and immediately called John, who at this point had found his way to Jacksonville, Florida, staying at his sister Jolene's house. I couldn't understand how she believed that bringing her brother and her addict husband together would be beneficial for either of them. John just kept using, even stealing pills and cash from his mother, who lived an hour away. I gave his sister so much credit for trying, at least. I felt sorry for her, understanding firsthand what kind of emotional pain she was likely experiencing.

"John, I just got off the phone with Pam Dalton and she told me everything. I mean everything." Click. He hung up on me. I kept calling back, but there was no answer. Finally, on about the third attempt, his sister Jolene answered his phone.

"Jolene, please let me talk to John. We were talking and he hung up on me."

"Steph, he is outside crying. He never wanted you to find out about Pam and his affair with her."

Bingo. There it was. The confirmation I had been waiting on for years. In one moment in time, decades of doubt became very clear.

I called Pamela back. "Pam, I just talked to John and he told me everything. Everything. Including about your affair with him."

"I'm so sorry, Stephanie, I didn't want you to find out about that. I thought I could just tell you what you needed to know without getting into specifics. I never meant to hurt you or intrude on your marriage."

"It's okay, Pam," I found myself saying. It was as if another being took over. I stayed calm and collected as I told her what an angel she was. I spent a lifetime with John, always looking over his shoulder to see if there was someone else there but never could prove anything, despite many suspicions over the years. His admission of their affair was the confirmation I'd been waiting to see for over two decades. I knew I couldn't ever face leaving him for adultery if I didn't know for sure it was going on. But I had a gut feeling that it was happening, despite the lack of evidence. Pam further shared that John had been having many affairs over the years. She wasn't his first, nor his last. He started cheating on her with a girl who worked at one of the HVAC supply shops, and that's when she broke off the relationship with him. No sooner than she'd done that, her husband, who discovered their affair, sued her for divorce on the grounds of adultery. He had the phone records of both Pamela and John subpoenaed as part of his case. John, paranoid about me finding out about their affair, arranged for his court subpoena to be delivered to an attorney's office rather than to our house. They obliged. He was shocked when he arrived at the law office to find that the assigned attorney was none other than Marvin Bates, the one who handled the case for us when Abi was bitten in the face by a neighbor's dog. Fate can be wicked.

Pam so kindly offered to let me see the results of her HIV tests she was getting every six months. *What the fuck?* It hit me — *there was probably even more to be concerned about.* She told me she got tested for HIV all the time, and would share her results with me.

"No, thanks," I responded. "I believe you. I guess I should go get myself tested, too."

The divorce was already final, so adultery was not in our final decree, but to be validated was huge for me. He could no longer make me feel crazy for suspecting him of having affairs.

I knew now. It had all been true. My gut feeling was that he was cheating, but he was so good at lying that I never had concrete proof. I knew to believe my gut. There was proof in all forms of media around me. I knew it instinctively. *So why the fuck hadn't I pursued it to its conclusion? Why did I just let myself buy into believing the lies so easily?* The cost now seemed insurmountable. *Was I fated to spend my older years alone because no one would want this old, damaged soul for a mate?* I was far more sensitive than people knew. I absorbed all of this pain and wondered how damn long it would take to process it and lock it away for good.

56
IS IT ON THE TABLE?

"The pain you feel today will be the strength you feel tomorrow." - Stephen Richards

Between the addict, my youngest leaving home for college, the divorce, my mother dying and finding out John had been an adulterer and substance abuser our entire lives together, it was too much. With such a doubtful future, I was losing all hope. Hope had kept me alive and wanting to live. Losing hope would be detrimental, and yet I couldn't seem to keep the losses at bay. I felt I had disappeared in all the chaos. My mother was gone. I'd have to move away and leave my job at the karate studio that I loved, losing my home and most of my belongings as well. My kids were both grown and doing so well in life. It would be a good time to exit stage left. I started seriously considering suicide as an option. *Why not?*

One Sunday at my Unity Church during Minister Connie's talk, I pondered long and hard about the ways I could off myself, particularly any ways it could look like an accident. I wouldn't want my kids to carry any guilt or shame over my suicide. As I glanced out a window, I watched an 18-wheeler drive by. *That may be the way. Walk to the nearby convenience store and gas station; walk slowly until an 18-wheeler comes along. Find something to trip on.* I felt at peace for a moment. I had a plan that could really work. *No one would have to know it was planned. It would appear to be an accident.* Prayers. Closing prayers. Okay, back to reality. They brought all the children in at the end of each service to help sing us out. Suddenly, I heard her in the distance.

"FEFFY!!!!!!!! THERE'S MY FEFFY!!!!!" she yelled out. It was Siren. My precious Siren, all of 3 years old, was hollering out through the crowd to get my attention. She wiggled out of the arms holding her and started running toward me. I was way in the back, so she had to push her way through dozens of people to get to me. The entire congregation turned to see who this "Feffy," was. Siren jumped into my arms, gave me an enormous hug and kiss, and then rested her head on my shoulder. I could feel the tears stinging my eyes and fought so hard not to bawl. *Siren still needed me. No one else out there actually needed me, but she did. I couldn't leave her. How selfish of me to even consider doing such a thing. My precious didn't deserve the hurt of her Feffy leaving her.* I vowed never to consider suicide again. It was not an option and had to be off the table. *Buck up, bitch. You've got work to do.*

57
ASHEVILLE BOUND

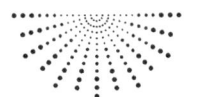

∽

"New beginnings are often disguised as painful endings."
- Lao Tzu

∽

The house was not selling, and I was getting panicky. I had enough money to last me until June 2001, but no longer than that. It was now April, and I was feeling the anxiety settle in for a stay until I could sell this place, pay bills, and leave. I had looked at staying in the area, but rents were so expensive, at least in any area I would have felt safe living in. My plan was to move to Asheville, North Carolina, so I could become a resident and qualify for Trevor's tuition to be in-state rather than the more expense out-of-state cost.

Taking a recommendation from Pamela, the mistress, I hired her old boss, JP Nelson of Nelson Realtors. JP was an older, affable, tall man with dark hair and a contagious smile. The first time we met, we sat outside on the back patio so I could smoke my cigarettes. To my surprise, JP pulled out a pack, and we sat there smoking cigarettes and talking real estate. I felt so comfortable with him and his ability to get my house sold. He exuded confidence. Thankfully, he came through with a contract no less than five weeks later. We had a closing date of July 22, 2001. Exactly one year, to the day, from when I had the locks to the house changed to stop John from stealing our belongings. One year and four months from the day I heard that word uttered: "cocaine." What a lifetime ago.

After successfully closing on the house, JP and I walked outside the attorney's office to say our thank you's and good-byes. Before I could get one out, he leaned over, draped his arm around the back of my head, and brought me to his lips for a full-on kiss. I was tight-lipped and stunned.

"I've been wanting to do that since the day I met you," he almost whispered. Too astonished to respond, I just muttered, "Thanks for everything. Good luck to you and good-bye." In a weird way, though, the encounter helped me begin to see that maybe I wasn't too old to find a life partner again. There might still be something desirable about me.

The movers had come and gone, and I went back to our house one last time to pick up my cockatiels, Kiko and Tiki. Gordy and Marie had hired people to come clean the house for me so I could get on the road. Their help meant the world to me. I had to pack the car and birds and leave Memphis. I was so incredibly sad to move away from my daughter, my grand-daughter, my family, my friends, my job, my karate family. That enormous, empty space would probably never be filled again in the same way. Sure, there would be new people, friends, and experiences coming along, but this last era had been good, and our future had looked promising. Now, the future held hard questions and hollow answers. *How would I support myself? Would I even be able to get a job in Asheville?* I tried to be optimistic, seeing it as a fresh start.

I stopped halfway in Cookeville, Tennessee, to spend the night and make sure I didn't wear myself out driving. I was never a good long-distance driver or rider. Secretly, I brought the birds into my room at the small, pet-free hotel near the highway. It was a tidy enough room. Sitting up in bed, watching TV, I decided now would be a good time to read the letter my brother Gordy had given me and asked me to read later.

I opened up the envelope to reveal the check I had written him with a heart cut out of the middle, rendering it invalid. I burst into tears. It was the best gift I could've ever gotten. My funds having run out, I had to borrow $2,000 from Gordy and Marie to pay the July mortgage and utility bills. I'd written him a postdated check that he could cash on the day of closing. This money, along with the closing funds, would see me through at least a year. I needed to find work right away in Asheville and would start looking as soon as I arrived.

The next morning, I got back on the road. It was a beautiful, bright, sunny day as I rode into Asheville on I-240 and breezed under the iconic "Welcome to Asheville" sign on the highway. I knew it would be a tough change, but one that could be full of endless opportunities and possibilities. I felt exhausted and yet ready. The healing blue mountains wrapped themselves around me. My hope coffers were filling back up again.

— The End —

POSTSCRIPT

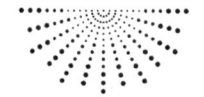

"Start now. Start where you are. Start with fear. Start with pain. Start with doubt. Start with hands shaking. Start with the voice trembling, but start. Start and don't stop. Start where you are, with what you have. Just … start." - Unknown

Today, Stephanie lives in Tennessee with her love, Mike, whom she met while living in Asheville, North Carolina. They share a beautiful home with two precious pups, a Maltipoo and a Havanese. Their family includes six adult children and five fabulous grandchildren! Her life has become magical, and she is overflowing with gratitude.

FINDING CONNIE

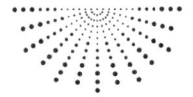

Please help me find Connie Fulbert (not her real name). Connie saved me, and I so want to thank her for that. I would love to see and express my gratitude to her in person.

If you think you know who Connie is, please send me her real name in an email, through one of the websites below. Thank you so much!

VestigesOfLight.com

StephPleasant.com

ACKNOWLEDGEMENTS

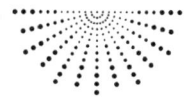

∽

"That best portion of a good person's life: his little, nameless, unremembered acts of kindness and love."
- William Wordsworth

∽

SPECIAL THANKS TO...
Alberta for loving and caring for me like a mom
Angelita for loving me so much
Coach Profesora for making me a track and field star
My teachers at The American Community School in BA
All my friends at ACS for caring about me
The woman coach at Ridgeview HS for believing in me and my athletic abilities
Jessica and the boys for loving me like family

The chef at The Torch and Candle restaurant for not shooting my father

Marilyn for being a good friend to me

The man who took me to lunch at the Rexall counter

Connie Fulbert for taking me into her home

Elsie for saving me from Chains

Mike for wanting to defend my honor

Mel for not allowing me to do porn movies

Nancy, the nurse from Boston

Lynn for allowing me to use her sofa bed

Ted Cantrell for calling his mother

Mama Cantrell for saving my life

The doctors and nurses at Grady Hospital who operated on me and saved my life

The doctor who came to my room every day to eat and keep me company

Martin and his family for teaching me so much

Ed Tant for caring

The German lady on the airplane who told me I was an exceptional mother

The bank lady for taking the time to show me how to reconcile a checking account

The trucker who took me home when I ran out of gas at 10 pm on I-75/85 north

Oprah for health, healing, and hope

Rob and my Karate family, including Catherine, Carolyn, Marvin, Mary, Gadson, and other great folks, for believing in me

Beth for her unconditional, selfless love and caring

Marie and Lucy for Friday lunch dates that kept me grounded

USAA for trusting me

Kathy G. for my beautiful paper Muse

Trevor, Abi, Tylur, and Kelly, for their enduring love

My grandchildren for their deep love and caring

Sage for loving and saving me

My extended family for their love and caring

My siblings for their love and support over the years

Sarah B., Chris S., and Layna for their enduring love and deep friendships

Bettye, Andy, Gary, Danny, Sean, Stephanie, Diane, Marilyn E., Val, Carolyn, Francine, Nancy, Shelby and Tawnee for their help, love, support, and encouragement

Mark Manson for his words full of wisdom and healing

Jenn and Terri for listening to me and keeping me presentable

Danny S. for his kindness and help

Steve B. for his invaluable feedback and input, saving me from myself

Charissa for her care, love, and guidance

AUTHOR'S MUSING

∼

"Memory is the diary that we all carry about with us."
- Oscar Wilde

∼

As readers may imagine, a memoirist cannot possibly recall all conversations from the past with perfect word-for-word accuracy, so we rely on reconstructed dialogue.

Reconstructed dialogue conveys the essence of a conversation, including the unique speech patterns and word choices of the individuals involved. One reference on the subject specifically recommended that the essence of the conversation be at least 80 percent true to the best of the writer's recollection. I am fairly confident that the gist of conversations relayed in this book are closer to 98 percent true.

Our beautiful brains have a way of crystallizing memories

that either cause us trauma or leave dramatic, lasting impressions. This safety mechanism allows us to connect quickly with memories of traumatic incidents if they recur, warning us in advance of potential danger.

So, while I may not remember what I watched on TV yesterday, I do not easily forget some of the more hurtful, frightening, or impactful interactions I have had with people. In the retelling of these events, I used reconstructed dialogue with confidence in the accuracy of my recollection.

I have also included memories shared with me through the years by my siblings, parents, and other close relatives. An extensive collection of family photographs, historical records, personal letters, and even some Wikipedia pages has provided further detail and sparked additional memories as well.

DISCLAIMER

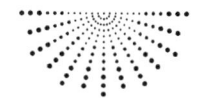

This work depicts actual events in the life of the author as truthfully as recollection permits, although a handful of details have been altered for the sake of storytelling. While all individuals mentioned within are actual people, some names and identifying characteristics have been changed to respect their privacy.